The World's Worst Entrepreneur

Aqil Radjab

Fisher King Publishing

The World's Worst Entrepreneur
Copyright © Aqil Radjab 2015

ISBN 978-1-910406-19-9

Cover design: Based on original work by Titus Vegter
Cover photograph: Speer Fotografie

Fisher King Publishing Ltd
The Studio, Arthington Lane
Pool-in-Wharfedale,
LS21 1JZ
England.

For Sascha, Emir
and Tygo

'The meeting of preparation
with opportunity generates
the offspring we call luck.'
Anthony Robbins

Contents

The World's Worst Entrepreneur

This is my own story, not a manual. It recounts my rise, fall and resurgence as a human being and as an entrepreneur. And it sets out basic principles, prerequisites and techniques for realizing the things that maybe you hardly dare to dream of. Just like I did. Whatever the case, it'll make you a better and happier person, I promise you.

Just a few years ago I was deeply unhappy. I had lost just about everything and felt I was the world's worst entrepreneur. I realized that the hopeless situation I found myself in was the result of the choices I had made. Short-sighted decisions that had totally destroyed the foundations of my life. But everyone makes decisions, after all, so how come mine had brought such disastrous results and consequences?

Instead of examining each individual decision I had made, I started looking for the reasons why I had made such decisions. Gradually I discovered that I could change things deep within me: intriguing, disturbing things that I hadn't even known existed, but which nonetheless made me do the things I did. So I decided to change and this change brought me the life I lead today. A full and happy life, in which I get the best out of myself and, I hope, out of those around me.

We all have the ability to give direction to our own life. We do it every day. We create reality in line with our self-image and we base our expectations on this. And we have the unlimited freedom to create ourselves and our future in accordance with an ideal we have in our mind.

What's my secret? A trio of gratitude, goal and direction. A sense of gratitude restored my strength and conviction to me after a difficult period, and the goal gave me my direction. Together, these things made me a better person and brought me financial independence.

I would like to express my thanks to everyone I encountered on my path, and also my gratitude for the mistakes I made.

Aqil

'WORK OUT WHY YOU WANT SOMETHING. THIS GIVES YOU THE MOTIVATION TO REALLY INFLUENCE YOUR OWN LIFE. THE REASON WHY DETERMINES THE STRENGTH AND DETERMINATION WITH WHICH YOU HEAD FOR YOUR GOAL. THE NEXT STEP IS TO DISCOVER HOW YOU WANT TO DO IT.'

A dream of success

Just imagine. At the exact moment you read this, you get the feeling that your life, your business, your love, your luck or whatever could and should be better than it is. It's your great, secret wish to improve your current situation or, even better, to pursue an ideal that, when you really consider it, is pretty damn ambitious. And of course that's why this wish is secret, because what would other people think about such a crazy dream, and what would they recommend you to do? After all, the others are just as smart as you.

So let me tell you it's possible. You can be happier and more successful than you are now. Or even happier and even more successful, if you're already doing OK. In your private life and in your business life.

And I can prove it.

Over the course of a few years I was privileged to receive three awards on behalf of the enterprise Payroll Company: the High Growth Award in 2009, the FD Golden Gazelle in 2010 and the FD Golden Gazelle in 2011. The names of these awards may mean nothing to you, but they are presented every year to the fastest growing businesses in the Netherlands, and mine was one of them.

In Payroll Company's founding year, 2005, it had a turnover of 400,000 euros. Five years later this had multiplied to around 12 million euros and since then the rising line has remained aimed at the skies. During these same years the labour market demand dropped, but we as a company never suffered from this. On the contrary. We were so recession-proof that, in proportional terms, we actually profited from it.

The success of Payroll Company was also my success. The company was my brainchild, I was its architect. I had conceived it and started building it with no money. My greatest capital had been my ability to dream.

So you can imagine how proud I felt to take the stage in three successive years, lifting the trophy above my head and being applauded by an audience of entrepreneurs. Cameras flashed and the next day my big beaming face would be in the newspapers. Close to the stage was my wife Sascha, watching me. I couldn't see her face but that didn't matter, because at that moment – as in every year – my heart was with her. In earlier, much more difficult times she had never blamed or accused me, while I had so much to accuse myself of...

Not so long before, my proud shining face had looked very different: tired, defeated and desperate. You see, Payroll Company wasn't my first company. Some years before creating this company I had decided to become an entrepreneur and had begun a staff leasing agency. It was called Extra Hands and was part of a franchise formula in which I was responsible for my own performance. I hired out myself and my thirty employees to clients for all kinds of technical tasks. And because it all went so well I was convinced I was a sensational entrepreneur.

Believe me, it's fantastic to be a sensational entrepreneur! When things are humming along you have the world at your feet, the future is bright, everyone smiles at you and you smile self-confidently back.

OK, sometimes things can get a little difficult and then you smile even more, because it's still full steam ahead.

Until it goes wrong.

Really wrong.

I went bankrupt and ended up in a debt restructuring programme. And not just me, but Sascha and our little sons Emir and Tygo, too. Why? Because it turned out I wasn't a fantastic entrepreneur after all, but a business idiot.

A friend of mine once wrote: 'a company is the reflection of the entrepreneur'. And that's how it was with me, too. On the outside, the business I had built up seemed to be going from strength to strength, but on the inside it was chaos which for a long time stayed hidden behind a successful facade – just like me. Was that a problem? Yes. Because my business activities weren't separated from my private life. Those who I loved most had to suffer the severe results of my bad entrepreneurship, along with myself.

Our furniture was carried out of the house, the children's saving accounts were emptied, the house sold and we ended up on the street with just the clothes on our backs.

How fantastic do you feel then?

As I write this I'm reliving the emotions of that time. The fear, the helplessness, the frustration, the desperation... But now I feel them without the destructive pain. The pain forced me to take a fundamentally different view of myself and my life. I had to change the things I saw, thought and did.

This 'different view' of myself, my life and the way I did things was no theoretical exercise. Nor did it involve simply weighing up the pros and cons and retaining what was good. The fear and the pain went too deep for that. In his book The Secret of Genius, Tijn Touber, the founder of the Dutch pop group Loïs Lane and today also an author of spiritual books, describes how Eckhart Tolle, a familiar name in the world of spirituality, underwent his transformation from panic-stricken man to reborn human being. 'He fears losing himself and – as his body starts to shake uncontrollably – he holds on desperately to who he thinks he is: he is Eckhart Tolle, researcher at Cambridge University, he is a German, he is a man, a human being, a… But it's already too late. The maelstrom takes him down into unfathomable depths and all he can do is let himself fall.'

My 'transformation' was less intense and uncontrollable, but nonetheless the comparison is justified. Because when Eckhart Tolle comes to himself, the world around him seems to have been changed. 'The sunlight coming through the curtains is so beautiful that tears come to his eyes.'

And I recognize the new world he saw.

As you read this, let's agree that there is something in your life, too, which could be different and better. Maybe we don't know what it is yet. You're the only one who knows why it should change. And this why is the most important thing at the moment, much more important than the how. Because first you need to know why you want something, and only then do you need to find out how you want to achieve it. Without the why you won't have enough motivation to really influence your own life. That's because the reason why you want to go somewhere determines the strength and determination with which you head for your goal.

What do you think will happen if I get into my car one morning, without any clear reason or motivation, to drive all the way from my home in the north of the Netherlands to a city in the south, more than

300 kilometres away? If I don't have a reason for going there, then it's likely that after just a few kilometres I'll start having doubts about my journey, abandon the idea, turn off the road and go and do something else. Because why in heaven's name should I spend three hours sitting in the car, driving across the country to go somewhere where I have no task or purpose? There's no reason for my journey, no why.

It would be completely different if I were to receive a telephone call. If I were to hear that my long-lost daughter has surfaced in that city, 300 kilometres away, and is now staying with friends. The only conceivable course of action in this case would be to jump into the car and drive flat out, full of determination, towards the south. What do I care then about not getting anything to eat or drink during the journey, or getting fined for speeding? Nothing at all, just as long as I can hold her in my arms. I would have a very powerful why for reaching my goal.

From my own experience, and with full conviction, I know that as you read these words you can decide to be happier and more successful than you are, or maybe even think possible right now. I know how you can find the right motivations and apply the right strength to realize a dream – be this a successful company, a trip round the world, a new existence, building an Ark, creating a vegetable garden or something else. I myself have shown that it's possible to imagine your ideal life as person or as entrepreneur, and then to make this idea reality.

This involves basic principles, prerequisites and even techniques. Before I could discover these I first had to experience intensely what it means to 'fail' and as a consequence to be desperately unhappy. I learned lessons from this, and then I showed that even after the greatest defeat you can use your shortcomings and your wrong decisions to achieve something better for yourself and for others.

Here's my message: everyone who wants to realize a dream can do it. This dream doesn't need to be business-related, but it can be. Just as long as it's your dream. But I don't give any money-back guarantee if you don't achieve your goals, because they are sure to keep changing the closer you get to them.

Do you know the best thing about all this? If even I can achieve my heart's desire, then you can certainly do it too.

How?

I'll tell you.

3

Sheikh Juma

My father is a descendent of the Circassians, a mountain people from the Caucasus who fought against the Russians for many years. When his people lost the struggle in the mid-19th century, they were given a choice: either come down from the mountains and submit to the new Russian rule, or leave the region. This triggered an exodus that scattered the Circassian folk and led to my ancestors settling in Syria, which at that time was still a province of the Ottoman Empire.

And so Menbedj was the place where my grandparents and my father were born. The village was governed by a spiritual leader, Sheikh Juma. If you wanted to know where rain came from, then this Sheikh Juma told you that an angel named Michael was somewhere up in the clouds with a pot of water and a soup ladle. Each time he scooped a little water from the jug and tipped it out and so this became a cloud that fell to earth somewhere as rain. My father often had to beat a drum and shout at the top of his voice to 'free the moon of its besiegers'. The besiegers were the devil, the giant, the whale or something like that. In reality it was an eclipse of the moon that came and went by itself. It all seems like childish naivety and infantile ignorance, but anyone who went against this sort of 'wisdom' could look forward to hell and damnation.

My father rejected this life of ignorance. What's more, as he told me, he found it inhuman that girls were married off and lost their virginity at the age of twelve. He attributed such wrongs and abuses to the interpretation of Islam which Sheikh Juma eagerly employed for his own ends.

In a bid to escape from the stifling reality in which he lived, my father decided to follow his dream and thus departed from his birthplace and roots. Heading towards an uncertain future, he left behind his family and his past. By way of Africa, Italy and Germany he then came to the Netherlands, where he studied biology in Leiden. One purpose of his studies was to prove for himself that the theory of evolution was valid, and in doing so to demonstrate the falseness of Islam and of Sheikh Juma. After graduating my father was employed as a researcher and while working in a hospital he met my mother.

My maternal grandfather was quickly impressed by my father's character and achievements but my grandmother, as a member of the strict Reformed Church, needed more time to accept an apostate Muslim from Syria, a descendent of the Circassians, as her future son-in-law in the small Zeeland community.

But nonetheless: all's well that ends well. My father and mother were in love, they got engaged, they married and I was born.

What I'm describing here is the very short version of an incredible life adventure. What an amazing achievement to change your future so radically and to begin a completely new life! You need a truly enterprising and resolute spirit to do that – and I'm not just saying that because it's my own father.

Radical life changes such as those experienced by my father are, when you look at the root causes, seldom motivated positively. Eckhart Tolle was caught in an emotional maelstrom that was the product of his deepest sense of desperation. Others commit a deed of life-changing foolishness – aggression, adultery – that stems from concealed dissatisfaction. And if you are satisfied with life as it is, or as it seems to be, what inner compulsion can you have to change course so radically?

I was fifteen when my parents moved from the west of the Netherlands to a farmstead in the north, a stretched-out hamlet with a church and a school, even smaller than Menbedj. It was certainly a nice, quiet place for my father and mother, but not so great for a teenager like me. Nonetheless, the move brought me something both unexpected and wonderful. I met a girl, Sascha, who turned out to be the love of my life.

But however liberated and unencumbered my father was, he had still brought his culture, norms and values with him from Syria. In the Netherlands he had seized the chance to educate and develop himself to far above the level of Sheikh Juma, the influential potentate who threatened people with the devil. So he viewed education as the ultimate thing in life. But I, his son, took few things seriously and school certainly wasn't one of them.

Two strong and individual personalities – my father and I – ended up opposed to each other, and matters came to a head. I left home and went to live in a little flat in a neighbouring village.

I was sixteen.

Things didn't get much better after this. I lost all interest in school, but found plenty of time for Sascha and for my personal freedoms. At night I went out drinking and gambling. I was a virtual stranger to the classroom, but I was a regular in bars and pubs. I acquired the wrong kind of friends and ended up in a police cell. But only for a short while, and not long enough to learn my lesson.

At school things quickly went downhill. I moved from a top-level grammar school to a comprehensive school, and then to another lower-level school which I barely managed to complete.

Sascha was getting worried. She got a job at a nursing home and took up residence in a nurse's flat, and I moved in with her. She got me out of the environment that seemed to be so bad for me.

This personal story is important because it reveals the kind of fool I can be. I wasn't an evil or stupid young guy, or so I think, but I was very stubborn and followed my heart and impulses rather than my head. I was also engaged in senseless activities. I didn't take any real pleasure in the things I did or see any sense in them, I didn't imbue these things with any sense, and so what I did was in itself senseless.

But above all I was reacting to my surroundings and my circumstances, and I didn't realize that I had the potential to influence these. It was events that kept me in motion, not my ambitions. Life and its changes happened to me. I underwent them. In the confrontation with my father my weapons were passive resistance and indifference. I also used these weapons as a way of protesting against whatever I had to endure. 'What do you mean, go visit my parents? What are you talking about, going to school? What's the point?' The advantage of these weapons was not only their effectiveness against those who loved me. There was an additional effect relating to myself and, as I later learned, my hidden fear.

It seemed that they prevented failure.

4

The failure factor

Do you know the game show Fear Factor? Until a few years ago this was a regular feature on TV. In the show the candidates are presented with physical and mental challenges where they have to overcome their fear and revulsion. One of the challenges is to eat live maggots, slugs and other protein-rich dishes. While watching you can feel them moving in your own mouth and throat.

That feeling of live worms twisting in my gut: I used to get it from something else. The thought of failure.

Failure was – and is – something terrible for me. It was a feeling in my stomach, my head and my whole being. Not that I realized this at the time, because when I was young I had a strong, but unconscious, defence mechanism. Passivity and indifference prevented me from being confronted with the feeling.

Inducing failure, however strange it may sound, is a safe option for not having to fail. Place yourself outside a system or give up your ambition, and then you don't have to perform to any real extent. If you don't have to perform well, then you can't fail either. Great logic, huh? The same logic seems to apply to expectations, too. If you don't expect anything, then you can't be disappointed either.

But there's a big problem that comes with this way of thinking. Expectations are often part of the pleasant sense of anticipation before an event, and thus put you in the mental state in which you can enjoy something. If you've planned an evening with your partner and/or with friends, then it's something you look forward to. You choose a nice outfit, put money in your pocket and walk into a restaurant with an expectant smile on your lips. The owner of the restaurant welcomes you as you hoped, the evening is a success and, as you were unconsciously expecting, you even get a free drink on the house. To a great extent, your prior expectations determine the success of the evening and thus also influence your expectations for the future.

Expectations have such a big effect on us that, as Dan Ariely writes in his book Predictably Irrational, they make placebos into effective medicines. In the chapter 'The Effect of Expectations' (subtitle: Why the Mind Gets What It Expects) he says that when we believe in advance that something will be good or tasty, then we experience or taste it accordingly. And if we think that it will be nasty or bad, that's how it is too. Expectations not only determine how we experience flavours (rating Pepsi or Coke, for instance) but also influence almost every aspect of our lives and shape our stereotypes of people and groups. In another chapter Ariely talks about 'The Power of Price'. Here, it seems that the price of a placebo, painkiller or energy drink influences the effect it has on us. It works better because we believe that it will work better. And we expect this effect because it's more expensive.

What applies to an evening out, to Pepsi, Coca Cola and placebos, applies to life as a whole. When you approach your future with a sense of expectation and pleasant anticipation, it will turn out correspondingly. Or at least that's how you'll experience it because you seek confirmation for this feeling and are open to it. Don't expect anything from life, and you won't fail or be disappointed. But life won't give you anything either.

Expectations are located in your head. They are a form of dreaming and a fruit of your imagination. Unfortunately, a fruit like this can be nipped in the bud. Be it love, career or life: for every positive change you imagine in these areas, fear of failure is what holds you back the most. Without you realizing it, fear of failure can lie at the root of every sensible argument that keeps you from following your dream. Combine the failure factor and the Fear Factor, and you get a game show with no candidates prepared to take part. Anybody who is unsure about his or her future success, thinks about it a while and has some self-control will then come up with enough reasons and arguments for not doing it. The risk is too great... What if it goes wrong... I'll be sacrificing too much for it... My husband or wife won't allow me...

If you keep presenting yourself with these and other seemingly sensible arguments for not moving off the familiar track in any way, then over the years you will prove yourself right. You will increasingly have things to lose, meaning that the risk also gets bigger in relative terms. You build a career, invest in a pension, and your financial dependencies increase. Realism sets the tone and the dream you once had is nothing more than that: a dream. And do you know what? Without any evidence to the contrary, without an alternative existence, then you're right too. The mind gets what it expects. And what about that evening out? No, better be sensible. Maybe tomorrow.

Despite all this, things can be different.

I once read an interview with Viggo Mortensen, the actor we all know from his role in The Lord of the Rings, where he plays the hero Aragorn, 'heir to the throne of Gondor and Arnor'. The article drew my attention with its title: Viggo Mortensen's fears. 'Feelings of fear are always a good benchmark for me,' said the actor. 'If it's a good script and I'm apprehensive whether I can manage the role, then I have to say "yes".'

So why say 'yes' to something that makes you feel afraid and involves the possibility of failure? Because fear is a great starting point for exploring and extending your boundaries. Because this fear tells you that you are moving off your familiar track, leaving your comfort zone, meeting the challenge, testing your abilities, etcetera. Or in other words: because you encounter and overcome the fear of failure so as to emerge better and stronger.

If you aren't aware of your own fears, then they will influence you in subtle ways. Because the fear remains hidden but steers your thoughts and your deeds. It can even argue against you with the help of a cunning interpreter: your own powers of logic.

Recognizing my fear of failure as the true argument against change and expectations gave me, in retrospect, a huge insight into my own life. Fear of failure was the biggest discouragement to my dreams. It was only when I acknowledged this fear that I was mostly able to free myself from it and start pushing back my boundaries.

5

'We'll call you Kevin'

A ship has a central passageway running fore to aft. In my case the ship was the H.M. Van Nes. I was nineteen years old and doing military service.

Life at sea seemed a bigger adventure to me than at home on the clay soil of the Northern Netherlands. A ship attracted me more than a nurse's flat. I was off to discover the world, and maybe myself too. OK, I'd more or less wasted my school years but the navy was giving me the chance to become a man. And moreover the navy was a way of escaping my continuingly purposeless and unemployed existence, while also allowing me to return home regularly – most importantly to Sascha.

In this central passageway there hung the 'P list', the 'placing list' with the names of everyone who boarded the ship or went ashore. I was on it. Seaman 3rd Class: A. Radjab. As a newcomer my task was to report directly to the caf-senior. 'Caf' was short for 'cafeteria', the Dutch term for crew accommodation.

Just as in prison, the crew accommodation on board a ship has a fixed hierarchy. Right at the back sat the biggest and thus strongest group: the technical department, nicknamed the 'stokers', a bunch of pretty tough guys.

'Hello, I'm Aqil Radjab,' I said politely after making my way through the cafeteria.

'But you don't look like a foreigner,' decided the caf-senior. He studied me and thought for a moment. 'We'll call you Kevin,' he said. 'Aqil is much too difficult.'

And so that was my name from then on: Kevin, seaman third class. I didn't have any training qualifications and I was right at the bottom of the hierarchy ladder. Just about everyone on board the ship was my superior and I had to follow every request by a superior like an order.

Once again, my decision to join the navy was a response to my circumstances, combined with the expectation of adventure. The decision to change my life hadn't been taken by me, but for me. I was subject to compulsory military service. Just for the connoisseurs: compulsory military service in the Netherlands was abolished in May 1997, so after this date no new conscripts were called up. But this was earlier, so I was conscripted.

In the seven years that I spent in the navy, I got to know the ports of the world. Cape Town, Miami, Shanghai, Stockholm… I specialized as a welder. Not that this was my dream job, but as a welder I had my own small room on board. I was more of a handyman than a specialist, but I learned on the job. And I started producing the ship's magazine, wrote columns and with my sense of justice and injustice I turned the spotlight on things that needed improvement. They called me 'Kevin the investigative reporter'.

About once every four months our ship returned to its home port, Den Helder. And each time Sascha stood waiting for me there. Each time we fell in love again. We got married.

Although I was pretty happy during those years, I had a low rank and had six or seven men above me who told me what to do. All day.

Before my time in the navy there had been just one man above me: my father, and that hadn't worked out well. But this time, having no choice, I learned a little discipline and responsibility.

But I was always struggling with a tricky issue, actually no more than a little word: must. It is word I prefer to avoid whenever possible (although you'll find it about 20 times in this book). 'Aqil, you must...' I don't even want to hear the end of that sentence. I already know that whatever I 'must' do, I am not going to do it. I've had this issue all my life, and all my life it's been a stumbling block for me. Which is pretty inconvenient and even unjust, because the word is often used by people around me who have my best interests at heart and who communicate in this way without knowing how allergic I am to that verb. And even though I understand that using that little word must is often nothing more than a habit, I'm still allergic to it. Even just a little bit of must is too much for me. Nobody tells me what I must do!

An allergy like this is a terrible problem for a seaman third class. Every day I had to obey almost everyone on the ship, and must applied to most things. In spite of everything I had learned about discipline and responsibility, that little word always made me sneeze.

It's an allergy that can be cured, of course, but I didn't want to cure it and I still don't. I prefer to live with the tricky consequences. Why? Because for me it means being an independent individual. When other people don't tell me that I must do something, it means that whatever I do, it's because I want to. As a choice, of my own free will.

Want is a stronger motivation than must. If you must work, then you count the days and years until retirement. If you want to work, then you get much more enjoyment from what you do. If you ask someone 'do you want to do this?', then the answer will be 'yes' or alternatively you'll find out in a quite natural way why he/she doesn't want this or that. And so you discover something you didn't consider before. Saying 'you must do this or that' is an admission of weakness. It gives you a surrogate importance with regard to the other person, because with this word you imply an objective and irrefutable rightness. And when you're communicating with yourself, it's the ultimate admission of weakness. It absolves you of responsibility and takes away part of your free will. 'I don't want to, but I must...'

Must is deeply rooted in our language and I think it's important to be properly aware of the word. I advise using it only when it describes a deep personal sense of longing. That's the only must we should want.

At a quarter to four in the afternoon in Den Helder it was end of shift. At half-past three all these big, grown-up guys were already standing with a suitcase in hand, waiting for the moment they were allowed to leave the ship. For years it hadn't bothered me, but now with each homecoming it annoyed me more and more. We were sailors, not civil servants!

I was sitting at the bar with two corporals. Just as in my younger years, smoking and drinking were my favourite activities.

'I only need to do another twelve years,' said one of the men, and suddenly I got a very bad feeling.

A sense of unrest and frustration was beginning to eat at me. Increasingly I felt that I had wasted my youth and somehow needed to make up ground. Wasn't this why I had gone to sea? It was the urge to prove to myself and others that I was good for something after all.

I didn't want to stay a sailor, but to show what I was worth. I wanted to be a captain and to start a family onshore. From seaman third class to captain? In naval hierarchy that was out of the question. OK, so I had secured a job for life, but all my life it would be impossible, or at least very difficult, to transcend my rank. This career limitation and all the musts in my life were frustrating me. I could never be a captain and so I decided I was going to be an entrepreneur. Then I would have all the freedom I needed and there'd be no-one to set me boundaries. No-one apart from myself.

How proud I felt when I decided to start my own business. That wonderful feeling of finally determining for myself who I would pay attention to, and above all who I would ignore. A long and glorious road to success lay before me. At last!

So I had to prepare. During the evenings at sea I took a distance learning course in General Entrepreneurship Skills and I visited the Starters' Day at the Chamber of Commerce. And I wrote a letter to my father, describing my plans to leave the navy and to start a career as an entrepreneur.

I was ready to go!

We were at sea for a long period that time, and the post was specially delivered to us on board by helicopter. Once the postbags were on board and had been sorted, a sergeant handed out the letters. Everyone who heard his name called came forward, grabbed his post and hurried off to his berth, a bunk bed with a little curtain. So did I, and to my great surprise there was a letter from my father. 'No news is good news,' was his motto, and so a letter from him was really something special.

I don't have the letter any more, but the essence was: 'My boy, don't do it. Your job is secure and will get you through life, so why risk it? You'll probably never find another job like this again...'

The letter hurt, but as I lay there in my berth I understood his words. For my father, education was the ultimate thing – and I had expertly flushed my education down the pan. He had had visions of me spending my life raking the leaves for the municipal gardens department. And moreover, he himself had tried his hand in the world of business several times, with financially disastrous results.

So I had mixed feelings about the letter, but thanks to my firm conviction and belief in my abilities I ignored his opinion and the essence of his message.

After all, when had I ever listened to him?

6

Here's Johnny!

Please be patient with my life story, because what I'm writing serves a purpose. I want to explain that you can be happier and more successful than you are, and that it's possible to realize a dream. That you shouldn't let this dream be blocked by so-called sensible arguments that are actually rooted in fear of failure. But I also want to tell you how foolish you are if you think a dream will just come true. You don't create and realize a dream by closing your eyes and setting off blindly. So long live fear, because it teaches you where the boundaries are between a dream and a possible nightmare. It can stop you taking a step that you regret later.

Like I did.

Deciding to be an entrepreneur was a big move for me, a radical life change. I was driven to it by fundamental dissatisfaction with my possibilities and by the prospect of many more years 'working shifts'. My life on board H.M. Van Nes had nothing to do with what I wanted and plenty to do with must. But ahead of me lay an enticing dream image, and I soothed my fear of failure with all the preparations I made. My father's fear of what might happen seemed to be stronger than mine.

Viggo Mortensen lets himself be guided by fear in a positive way, and Sheikh Juma mixed it with ignorance to create a crippling cocktail for his followers. Fear and ignorance amplify each other. Fear of the dark, because all you can see are your own ghosts. Fear of a future in which you might fail.

But what is fear?

Fear in its naked and primitive form is a basic reaction which involves the entire body, including the head. Blood flows away from your brain, adrenaline pumps through your body, your choices are freeze, flee or fight – although they are not really choices because you don't reason logically: now you're driven by instinct. Our basic urges are still anchored strongly within us, wired into our brain and our genes.

Of course, no-one likes to admit that their life is ruled by fear. Not to others, and above all not to themselves. One important reason is that the fear as such is not recognized. You only perceive it when it really comes to the surface. If you're sitting by the campfire, in the cinema or reading an exciting book, then the adrenaline gives you a kick without you having to experience the negative side-effects. That's recognisable fear, with a laugh or sigh of relief to banish it again.

But most fear remains hidden and is denied. It's the fear that lies concealed under a thin layer of well-argued logic and self-delusion. It hides within us, gazing out at the nasty outside world like a primitive reptile from under a stone. And so fear, although we don't really perceive it, is one of the great determining factors in our life, and no-one knows this better than advertisers. The book Brandwashed ('Tricks companies use to manipulate our minds and persuade us to buy') by the marketing guru Martin Lindstrom devotes a good chapter to this: 'Panic and paranoia: Why fear sells.'

In my following summary of contemporary fears, I have drawn my inspiration from Lindstrom.

We fear losing our job. We fear that our relationship will fail. We fear that someone else is better at doing our job than we are. We fear growing old. We fear that we won't grow old. We fear illness. We fear for our pension. We fear choices because these change the situation we know. We fear being faced with even more choices, because the more choices we have the greater the chance of a wrong decision. We fear the sense of fear.

With so many hidden fears, is it surprising that you don't find it easy to make decisions? Of course not. Fear, this primitive force within us, has ensured that we're still here today. Our fellow homo sapiens in prehistoric times who threw a handful of red berries into their mouths with no fear, and who came running when they heard a tiger roar in order to see how big and hungry the beast was – they have long been fossilized, leaving no descendants.

So fear makes us think about things before we start, and helps to prevent rash and reckless action. You're a fool if you know no fear, but you're a hero if you overcome it. And you're wise and on the path to happiness and success if you are able to recognize it - not just fear of failure, but all those little, hidden fears in our system that prevent us from seeing ourselves and the world around us in a neutral way. So that we can do the things that do us good, and which can make us even happier and more successful than we already are.

There was a time when I thought: if only I had been less expectant and instead a little more fearful. There was a time when I thought: if only I had remained a seaman third class. If only I had heeded my fear – and my father's advice.

'REALIZE THAT YOU ARE RESPONSIBLE. BECAUSE WHO YOU ARE, WHERE YOU STAND AND WHAT YOU'VE ACHIEVED SO FAR IS A DIRECT CONSEQUENCE OF THE CHOICES YOU MADE. THEY WERE MADE FOR DIFFERENT REASONS AND THEY HAD DIFFERENT OUTCOMES, BUT WHATEVER FORM THEY TOOK, THEY ALL HAD ONE THING IN COMMON: THEY WERE YOUR CHOICES.'

7

Hotshot entrepreneur, that's me

On 1 January 2000 I entered the world of business. The correspondence course in General Entrepreneurial Skills, which I had taken in my evening hours in the navy, gave me a sense of preparedness and confidence. What's more, in order to boost my chance of successful entrepreneurship even further I had attended the Starters' Day at the Chamber of Commerce. And to limit the risks even further, sensible lad that I was, I had decided that joining a franchise option was a safer option than starting a completely new company. After all, a franchise formula has a tried-and-tested concept and certain tasks are taken off your hands. So as a budding entrepreneur I had looked at plenty of options, from pizzas to shoes, and had decided on Extra Hands.

The logic of my decisions was indisputable.

Since 1991 Extra Hands had been supplying technical services and technical facility management services, specializing in areas such as metalworking, installation, electrical engineering, building construction, stand construction and interior design, focusing on fitting and installation companies as clients. You can still read about it on the website denationalefranchisegids.nl. The franchisee pays a starting fee and subsequently a seven- percent franchise fee and a three-percent marketing/advertising fee.

I was twenty-eight and I started making phone calls from my bedroom. I hired myself out for all kinds of technical work that I had learned in the navy. It turned out that were was plenty of work, and not only for me. I began signing work contracts: for a year and for indefinite periods. After just one year of entrepreneurship I was employing no less than thirty people. And I felt FAN-TAS-TIC. Wow, I was such a hotshot entrepreneur! Look at all the money I was earning!

With this money I started leading a life to match. I wasn't selfish. I bought clothes and cars for my employees and put just about everything I earned back into the business. The company flourished, and went from strength to strength. I attributed this to myself and my entrepreneurial qualities. Yup, things were going fantastically. I was fantastic. I appointed my best technician as salesman and I appointed the wife of one of my employees as bookkeeper. The outstanding payments from my customers started to mount up, but if I was temporarily short of cash I could always just go to the bank.

In particular, I was now profiting from one important piece of advice by the Chamber of Commerce: start a sole proprietorship, because it brings more tax benefits than a private limited company. For romantic reasons my marriage with Sascha had a community of property. And as an entrepreneur I left it that way, because my wife and I still felt just as romantic as during my navy days.

After two years I felt like a king and I had yet another good idea for further growth: I opened a second branch.

I was a brilliant businessman.

I thought.

But while my company seemed successful, I was blind to my own shortcomings. I thought that just about all my decisions were correct and sensible and that the growing turnover proved me right. But was that really the case? My best technician as salesman? Keeping the books as a part-time job? Well so what, who was going to contradict me? Where were the facts to prove me wrong?

I guess that in a time of success it's difficult to imagine a different future, or even to desire it. Certainly when you attribute the success to yourself it's hard to believe that it could all go wrong. After all, to believe that you need to have doubts about yourself, and how can you doubt yourself when you're so successful? The issue is even more difficult when you suffer from a hidden fear of failure. Taking a critical look at yourself then feels like criticizing yourself. And that's threatening.

Was the downfall that followed an unavoidable result of my lack of experience, of my intellect or my forecasting skills? Did I first have an incredible amount of good luck, and then an incredible amount of bad luck? Could I have seen disaster coming?

It wasn't until years later that I asked myself these questions, to which I now know the answers.

What do you think?

8

What if...?

What if, on 11 September 2001, two aeroplanes had swooped past the Twin Towers of the WTC with roaring engines, but without touching the buildings? If a few brave passengers had forced the hijackers of an airliner above Shanksville, Pennsylvania to land the aeroplane, and if a fourth airliner had flown just over the Pentagon in Washington without crashing?

Stock market prices wouldn't have fallen, losses wouldn't have been suffered, neither personal nor financial ones. And me? I might have achieved quicker success with my first enterprise. And instead of going financially, privately, morally and mentally bankrupt, I might have won the High Growth Award early in the new millennium. And then, with a triumphal grin of self-assurance and self-righteousness, I would have delivered a fine explanation for my success, which no-one could have contradicted because, after all, I was successful. Then I could have said, for instance, that the success was thanks to my correspondence course in General Entrepreneurial Skills or to the Starters' Day at the Chamber of Commerce. Or I might have said that my years at sea had finally taught me the discipline necessary to be successful, or that I was a decent and generous entrepreneur for whom my employees would go through fire and water, which was why we all performed so well together.

Everyone would have believed me, including myself.

But what would they have believed in? In my success-generating entrepreneurial skills, which might have been a result of the economic upturn at that time? Or in me and in my success, which lent credibility to every word I said?

If you are successful, you always reason backwards from the fortunate situation in which you now find yourself. And thus retrospectively create a recipe for success that sounds credible even if expressed in general terms, and which won't – indeed can't – be received with scepticism. You are successful, aren't you, so you must be right. Then it's enough just to describe the key points or point to the mistakes you avoided making, without really explaining why and how.

Can success be reasoned out in advance? Or indeed: is there a recipe for success and is it universal?

No, I don't think so.

As a consciously living person it's certainly possible to reason out an approach before you start, and to correct and optimize it as time passes, but this means taking a descriptive approach, which will be different for everyone. All people, all entrepreneurs and all companies, together with their circumstances, are different and, what's more, they certainly don't all want to achieve the same kind of success. Some want to just make a living with their little business, while others strive to build an empire. And you can also find enterprising people who want to make things happen, but not in a business context. How about being the first person to circle the globe in a balloon, or to descend to the deepest point of the ocean? Let's imagine something even crazier: how about a nice little house with a lovely wife and two lovely children? Now that really would be something special.

What if I had recognized the signs earlier? What if I had intervened more quickly?

But on 11 September 2001 two aeroplanes did fly into two high-rise buildings, and everything changed. Many projects were put on hold, meaning that fifteen of my thirty employees sat at home doing nothing. I had to save money, and I also needed money. I could apply for permission to lay off the guys sitting at home on economic grounds, but to do that I had to submit figures. Figures? I didn't even know where all my invoices were. And as soon as I went looking for them, I found all kinds of incoming bills floating around. It seemed that in the past I had made rather less profit than I thought. The stress increased, as did the payment deadlines.

But luckily I could always borrow money from the bank.

Because I had to dismiss my employees the unions got involved. Angry employees came to my door, and if they didn't then their wives came instead. I myself fell further and further behind with payments, received more and more visits from bailiffs, the fines got bigger and property seizures started to happen. Every time the telephone rang a cold hand gripped my heart.

All this happened to me. While I'd been doing my level best, and also had the best intentions for all those involved. And now they were treating me like a criminal! I was angry, miserable and aggrieved. Why me?

After four months of this the district judge issued a verdict. I was indeed allowed to dismiss fifteen people. But I had to pay their wages for two months more.

If you put a frog in a pot of cold water and slowly heat it up, then the frog won't jump out. I stayed where I was too. My debts to the bank had now risen to 200,000 euros and they wouldn't lend me any more. At least my house still functioned as limited collateral, so I was able to keep paying the wages. I tried borrowing money everywhere: from friends and acquaintances, from my parents.

Oh, how right my father had been in his letter...

Because I was so busy trying to sort out figures, money and documents, I hardly managed to acquire any new contracts. It was impossible to think about strategies and visions because all my time was taken up with tackling the consequences. I still didn't understand that my business model was flawed, and had always been flawed. Nor did I understand that I myself was striving for happiness and success in the wrong way. And it seemed too late for insights anyway. I was busy putting out fires while surrounded by flames and showers of sparks.

The same economic crisis that I believed was affecting me had shut down a number of my customers. As a result, I lost out on around 150,000 euros of invoices that were owing to me. And soon another six of my remaining fifteen employees were sitting at home, too. And once again I had to apply for permission to dismiss them.

All the misery started up again – but even worse this time. Once again the unions would intervene and once again the district judge would have to issue a verdict. The chilly hand around my heart grew even colder and the grip more powerful.

I hadn't kept up my mortgage payments, my credit card was exhausted; I had dismissed my employees and sold the tools.

I couldn't go on any longer.

It was my 9-11, in 2003.

In my capacity as a sole proprietorship I applied for suspension of payment.

I, the hotshot entrepreneur, was bankrupt.

I lost everything.

My company.

My home.

Myself.

Everything.

9

Everything I do is a failure

It was a long drive home. I had to tell her.

We sat down together.

'The bank is going to sell our house.'

'And what then?' she asked in dismay. There was panic in her voice and her eyes.

'I don't know,' I answered.

'Where are we going to live?'

'I don't know...'

We had two small sons, Emir and Tygo. The older boy was one-and-a-half, the younger boy was still a baby.

'I'm useless. Everything I do is a failure,' I cried out, and burst into a flood of tears.

Sascha hadn't asked for anything. She would have been happy with what we had, but I simply had to have more. And now I was dragging her and our children down into my pit. I had brought disaster on us all. Because my company was a sole proprietorship and our marriage had community of property, it wasn't just me who went under, but them as well.

All our names were in the newspaper. First all our stuff was carried out of the house. And then our house was sold.

And when I thought it couldn't get any worse, it got worse.

My children's' savings accounts were part of the estate assets and the administrator had them emptied, too.

That moment was like a punch to my face. A slow-motion one like you see in films.

I was knocked to the floor.

My total personal debt – and thus also the debt of my wife and children – was in the order of 400,000 euros. I was placed in a debt restructuring programme and I was required to relinquish everything I might earn. And from now on everything that Sascha earned went straight to the debt repayment, too. Moreover, she was actually obliged to keep working, meaning that we had to pay a child-minder ourselves. But how?

The bankruptcy hit me in the core of my being. Fears and worries crept out of their caves and my business failure didn't just eat at me, it devoured me. And not only me, but also those who I loved most.

My life was in chaos. The disruption felt physical, like searing pain. By now I didn't even have the strength to be angry with myself, or with the world that had abandoned me. Angry? I had messed it all up myself. I was wounded, numbed and afraid.

I felt ashamed because I wasn't able to support my family. There wasn't enough money to cover the basic necessities of life, and I had simply no idea how I was going to solve this. Would I even be able to solve it? After all, I had demonstrated my inexpertness as an entrepreneur and I was no longer able to direct my own financial affairs. What use was I then?

I wanted to run away, away from the place where I had lost everything. I wanted to disappear from the scene of my failure, where – to the disgrace of myself, my family and everyone who had trusted me – I had squandered everything I thought I had built up in the preceding years. I wanted to get away from the constant stress, from the sense of failure and from the shame.

I wanted to get away from myself.

10

The Naked Ape

Who you are, where you stand and what you've achieved so far is a direct consequence of the choices you made. Some of these choices may have been impulsive and unconsidered, some may seem to have been the result of your age or circumstances, a few turned out to be wrong in retrospect and others were brilliant. They were all made for different reasons and they had different outcomes, but whatever form they took, they all had one thing in common: they were your choices.

Of course, sometimes you were unlucky and sometimes things worked out great, but your current level of success or happiness, at this moment, doesn't depend on these external factors. It depends solely on the way in which you live and have lived, and on the decisions you take and have taken. Or the decisions you have not taken, for that matter, because actually they are decisions too.

My decision to become an entrepreneur was having dramatic consequences. I had done something very foolish in relinquishing what was secure and giving myself over to forces over which I had no control. And so the bankruptcy had happened to me. One moment I seemed to be successful, the next it turned out I was a failure. And all that because of two aeroplanes and two towers.

Or at least that's how I reasoned it.

Complete bullshit, of course.

It really hadn't been the aeroplanes, it had been me. I and I alone had taken the decisions that had led to me going bankrupt. And however logical these decisions had seemed to me at the time, they had been the result of an instable personal basis and motivation. My actions had been an accumulation of reactions. The combination of my lack of education and military conscription had led to my life as a sailor; the limitations of my role as a seaman third class together with my growing frustration had prompted me to become an entrepreneur. I had always reacted to events and circumstances instead of steering my own course. Of course, it had looked as if I was in control. After all, I was the one who decided to go to sea and then to return to a life on land. But what had this decision actually been based on?

In retrospect I can say for sure that many of my decisions as an entrepreneur were impure. My motive for success – the why – the method, and the goal were all flawed. That's because my motive was my ego. I wanted to be a success in my own eyes and in the eyes of others, and so I had a lot to prove and even more to lose, namely my self-esteem and my self-image. I didn't have any experiences of success in my childhood and youth to back me up. What would happen if I wasn't able to prove I could be a successful entrepreneur? Then it would prove the contrary: that I was a loser.

The method I applied and the choices I made were prompted by this faulty motive. And so the growth of my company led chiefly to the growth of my ego, and I wasn't able to look at the negative aspects in an objective way because these undermined my self-image. I wanted to prove myself and so I grew. Every growth in the form of money, employees or a new branch confirmed my success. My generosity was a further proof of how well I was doing. And when things went well, I attributed this to myself. I was increasingly unable to see any failings in myself because everything confirmed the rightness of my decisions, didn't it? And I avoided anything that pointed to failure, such as self-criticism or sobering figures in the accounts. I hadn't included a worst case scenario in my preparations and refused to consider one as time went by. I was scared to death of failure, so I banished that option from my mind.

Finally, my goal was wrong as well, because I had defined it on the basis of the same motive. I dreamed of my business career in the way you might dream of an ideal woman, with marriage then proving a bit of a disappointment. It can be frustrating to use your dream and your imagination in this limited way. But this was a limitation I imposed on myself for years.

Who was I, where did I stand and what had I achieved? No-one, nowhere, nothing. I was furious. To hell with it! Stupid idiot! Bastard! I've had it up to here! I cursed, raged, swore and wept. I completely lost it. The pain was so great. I was angry with the choices I had made. If I was anything or anyone, then at best The Naked Ape, exposed to merciless self-criticism and to all the threatening influences in my surroundings. My hiding place, my protective clothing and the instruments I had to protect myself, such as money and status – all gone. I felt cut off from normal, conceivable reality and I was overwhelmed by what had happened to me.

Every form of self-deception had been stripped away. All I had left was myself, but without self-respect that wasn't much. And I mistrusted what remained. Now that I had failed so massively, it seemed to me that my entire life, all my dreams and my identity were a lie. Everything I was and I had done was open to doubt. I was certain that I had failed, had been found wanting. I was convinced of my failure. The future that lay before me would be a grim extension of my unsuccessful past, while the present moment hung somewhere in between.

I had no idea where things could go from here. But I did know how much I had been injured, impaired, damaged. My business, my house, my money: it was all gone. I was miserable, angry, tired, ashamed, baffled, broken. In this state of mind, in which all seemed lost, I trudged up the stairs…

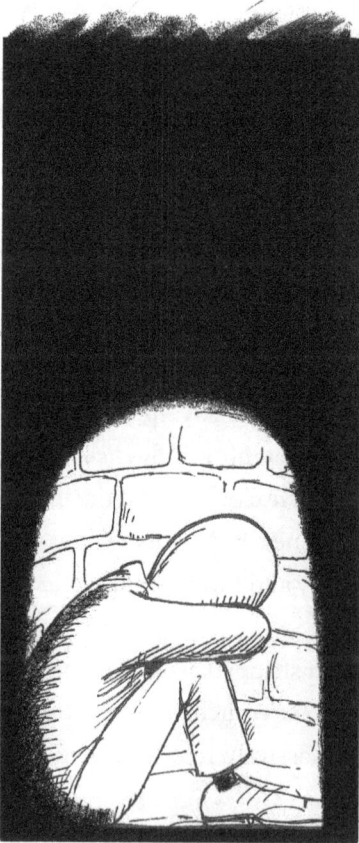

11

Little white socks

I trudged up the stairs. At the top stood the laundry basket and on top lay two little white socks. They belonged to Tygo, my son.

A sudden, almost shocking wave of gratitude and joy flowed through my body. If I can be happy in this moment, I realized, then it must always be possible.

It was an insight that changed everything.

Those two little white socks on the laundry basket made me realize that I had a wife who loved me as I was. That we were healthy and had two little children together, and that nothing could divide us. That we could lose everything, but would always have each other. So what was there really to lose? And what had I truly lost, if I still had the things that were most important to me?

Imagine darkness. In this darkness you suddenly see a little light. Only when you see the light do you become aware of the darkness, and know that there's something more. Not only now, but also still to come in that future of fear and uncertainty.

That is hope. And hope is a reason for happiness and gratitude. Not later, but now. Not there, but here.

Whoever you are, wherever you stand and whatever you've achieved: you can be happier and more successful than you are and realize the dream you want. Gratitude gives you the strength and conviction to do it. Do you think that sounds soft and squishy?

'Gratitude is such a powerful intention because it lets you experience that everything is already good right now. You are already healthy, rich, happy, brilliant and enlightened. You don't need to do anything to achieve something. It's all there already. This healing information is then reflected in every water molecule of your body, letting each cell align itself with those healing frequencies.' – Tijn Touber in The Secret of Genius.

'REALIZE ALL YOUR REASONS FOR BEING GRATEFUL. WITHOUT THIS REALIZATION YOUR LIFE WILL BE GOVERNED BY DISCONTENT AND YOU WILL HAVE NEITHER THE PASSION TO ACHIEVE WHAT YOU WANT NOR THE WILL TO DREAM. OF COURSE THIS DOESN'T MEAN GAZING INTO NOTHINGNESS IN PURE RAPTURE, BECAUSE A CERTAIN AMOUNT OF DISSATISFACTION MOVES YOU TO ACT. JUST NEVER FORGET TO BE GRATEFUL.'

12

The importance of being grateful

Never before had I experienced the sense of gratitude and joy so intensely. It was like a huge impulse of love that tore open my chest. A wonderful pain that suddenly let in all the light and love that I had radically shut out for so long – you see, I had been pushing away as many emotions as possible for fear of being overwhelmed by them.

I know it sounds dramatic, like a religious revelation. But I really was deep in the pit, and the experience was so intense. I'm also aware that gratitude doesn't seem the most heroic term or attribute that you can possess or acquire. The word tends to be associated with submission and not with victory. The Bible uses terms such as 'gratitude' and 'thankfulness' around five hundred times, for instance. 'You must be grateful, humble and small,' sang an old Dutch balladeer, and actually meant the opposite.

But there you are: if you're grateful, you really are happier and you think, see and judge more positively. Without a sense of gratitude your life will be governed by discontent and you will have neither the passion to achieve what you want nor the will to dream.

But isn't gratitude actually a form of acceptance that prevents you from really striving for something? Yes, if all you do is feel thankful for things, then it is. Then you'll just stare happily at the ceiling and nothing will happen.

I don't mean that kind of gratitude.

The gratitude I mean is true gratitude. The kind that makes you burst into tears. Tears of joy and not of self-reproach.

Tears falling on the laundry basket.

My gratitude was like suddenly falling in love, an emotion that didn't recede again and that took root like true love does. It was a sincere, deeply felt gratitude. At some moments it can still feel as powerful as the first falling in love that precedes true love and that never completely disappears.

Besides the huge gratitude for what I had, I also discovered gratitude for what was still to come. I was suddenly able once more to dream, to make plans and to act. It didn't just feel as if the door to the future had been opened for me, but as if an entire wall section had been removed. It was such an enormous contrast to the way I had seen myself and my problems over the years! The perspective was so different! The problems, the worries, the misery had been so big that they had stifled my perception of the world. Or was it me who had made them so big? While I sat there, exploring my new emotions, I started to realize that the latter was true. I had allowed the problems to gather above my head like dark clouds and to blight my whole existence. My financial situation cast a shadow on every area of my life. My health was suffering, my domestic situation, the way I interacted with friends and acquaintances, and my general view of the past, present and future. And because I had allowed this shadow to spread over me, I regarded myself as a helpless victim.

But what was the bottom line?

I was responsible for the company I had set up.

I was responsible for my mistakes.

I was responsible for the consequences.

I myself was responsible.

No-one else but me.

The little white socks brought me gratitude and joy. They gave me a new insight and plenty to think about if I wanted to express this insight in words and to see and place my former self, my past, present and future in a different perspective.

If I can be happy now, then this should always be possible.

If something as simple as this comes to you in a split second, can you call it an insight? I say you can. It was an illuminating insight that completely changed my view of the world. And as soon as I had gained this realization and started applying it, things in my life started happening fast.

Is it something unique, to have an illuminating insight like this, or to experience such a radical change in your emotions? No, because it can happen to you in many ways and at many moments. You're feeling worn out and apathetic, suddenly you receive good news and all at once you're smiling and full of energy.

In this case the change comes from outside, just as in my case with the white socks. The great thing is that you can create this shift to gratitude and happiness from the inside too. You don't need to wait for gratitude and happiness, you can choose them. And you don't need any special resources to do it. Even though we often think that we need certain things in order to be happy – a new TV, enough money or leisure time – that's not the case. Happiness is already there, in us. All we have to do is think of it.

The advantage of this approach, of course, is that you no longer depend on external factors and chance events to feel gratitude and happiness. They only lead to instable and short-lived happiness anyway.

Imagine a life in which you are grateful and happy only for short moments, and that each time you have to recreate this happiness and sense of gratitude by chasing after new goals. Is this a life that will bring an enduring feeling of contentment? Not in my view. But nevertheless that's how I lived my life for years. Engaged in a fervent quest for happiness and financial success. I chased after goals and in the process failed to realize that I didn't need to achieve happiness through these goals, because I already had it.

The white socks made that clear to me.

You need to be grateful NOW in order to achieve success. Why?

Gratitude results in calm, trust, strength, energy and conviction. It gives you a foundation for thinking and acting in the right way. It enables you to strive for true goals and to enjoy doing it.

Without gratitude you won't be able to recognize happiness and what's more, there's no point in striving for future goals, because you don't even know what will make you happy. You'll take the wrong path ('Once I'm rich, then I'll be happy'), or experience nothing but dissatisfaction on your path ('Is that all? Did I give my utmost just for this?').

Suppose I hadn't set up Payroll Company and had done something else instead. Would I then have been less happy?

The answer is a definite no. Because I realized that I was already happy when I started the process. Quite simply because happiness and gratitude are indispensable for this process, and ultimately they are not part of the goal you achieved.

According to Ben Tichelaar, 'Money is always a result of happiness and happiness is never a result of money.' Your happiness and gratitude should never depend on the goals you hope to achieve in the future. And I know that, because I was unhappy.

You may have noticed that in my experience, gratitude and happiness are very closely related. If I'm happy about something, then I'm also grateful for it – and vice versa.

So what is happiness?

For me, happiness is an awareness that I can tap into at any moment on any day. It's an active realization of what gives me joy right now. This joy can make me contented and grateful. What's more, it is something I can repeat. Seen from this perspective, happiness means regularly devoting myself to the things that make me a more joyful person. I can also work towards happiness, for instance by deciding to focus my time and energy on the things that give me joy, and organizing my life accordingly.

So how can I make a start with this? Or how can you?

Simply name three things that make the corners of your mouth turn upwards. They will form the foundation of your happiness. Say them out loud and really think about them. Envisage them in front of you, feel them. With this awareness you shift into a totally new emotional state. That's happiness, simple as that. If you can evoke these feelings of happiness, then you can move to the next stage: start working in the direction you want to go.

Is it difficult for you after all? Then try this one: The Flemish author Leo Bormans, approaching the phenomenon of happiness in a highly practical and applicable way, has written The World Book of Happiness on the subject. Here's one of his observations: turn up the corners of your mouth and try to think something negative. You'll find that it's not possible. And so you can conjure up happiness on a small scale simply by raising the corners of your mouth.

This is what I do: every day I say out loud what makes me happy, and the flow of life continues.

13

Dreams of home

I had lost my house and I had no idea what my future might look like. But thanks to my rediscovered sense of gratitude I could see a prospect that I hadn't had in the preceding years. Due to the bankruptcy verdict I was in a debt restructuring programme. The debts that remained after three austere years under administration would be cancelled and my family and I would receive a bankruptcy discharge certificate. It would all finally be over. This still didn't mean I could reconcile with myself, but my self-loathing was receding. For the first time in a long, long time I achieved a state of calm and emptiness in my mind. My ego had collapsed and crumbled, my view of myself and everything around me had lost its power, and my anger, pride and ambition had mostly evaporated. The hotshot entrepreneur was no more; all that was left was Aqil, but I wasn't too sure who that was.

While I was still in this first stage of calm and emptiness, a friend invited me to attend a visualization session he was leading in a Buddhist centre. I thought it would be a kind of imaginary journey which I could undertake in complete peace, a short mental holiday. And because I no longer had any judgements and prejudices, or anything to lose, I was able to give myself up to it completely.

It was wonderful to free myself of the chains of reality.

There, at the Buddhist centre, I imagined to myself what I would need to be happy again. I pictured a life in which I was prosperous, healthy and strong. A flourishing family around me, with everything they needed. I was the breadwinner and had reason to feel proud.

At that moment of the vision, the loss of our house appeared to be the most painful. I had financed this house, now lost due to my bankruptcy, from my carefully saved navy pay. It was my dream house on land, earned brick by brick during my seven years at sea. (I'll skip over the fact here that it was Sascha's house too…)

So I imagined a house, free of debt so that the bank could never get hold of it and never take it away from me again. I drew this house on a flip chart. A childish drawing: a square with a pointed roof. There were arrows going into it and arrows coming out of it. The ingoing arrows were income, safety and emotional security, with happiness, contentment, enjoyment going out.

I evoked the images and feelings that went with this house, which on paper was limited by my childish drawing abilities but in my head was painted in the glorious colours of the imagination.

I closed my eyes and stood about twenty paces from the house. In front of me was a drive of white gravel, the kind in which I loved to play when I was a child and which makes a nice sound when you walk on it. I walked with a soft crunching noise up the drive to the front door, through which I entered a spacious hall containing a wooden staircase leading upwards. There was a mirror in the hall and I paused in front of it. When I looked in the mirror I saw myself: happy, upright posture, strong and healthy. The house showed me as I would be then, in this other, imagined future.

I took a deep breath and walked up the stairs, keeping hold of the handrail. I knew that to the right, in Sascha's room, there would be a big walk-in wardrobe full of new clothes. At the time I was making this imaginary journey, my wife hadn't been able to buy any new clothes for two years, and my imagination seemed to realize how terrible I found this fact. I saw the children's bedrooms in front of me, arranged by the boys themselves and with the walls painted in the colours they had chosen. The bathroom, opposite the stairs at the end of the landing, had a spacious, raised bathtub that you seemed to sink into as soon as you stepped into it.

The attic contained a guest apartment with its own bathroom, so that friends could always stay the night in the house. And there was an exercise room where I could work out in winter and so keep myself in shape.

After I had walked through all these rooms in my imagination, and stored the images as memories in my mind, I went back down the stairs.

The living room on the ground floor was one big open space where Sascha, the children and I could spend time together and where we could cook and live. There was a TV corner with huge, cosy sofas where we could cuddle up together, a big wooden dining table we could all sit around and an open-plan kitchen so that we were always together, even when one of us was cooking.

Next to the living room was my home office, also functioning as a play area for the boys. The layout and furniture were based on the office of Maxwell Sheffield, a rich Broadway musical producer in the TV series The Nanny, which was first broadcast in the nineties. ('Oh Mr Sheffield! You wanna play that game? OK! You're the boss and I'm the nanny, you give me a raise, and I'll give you one!'). The room contained a wooden desk, a couch and a globe, because I love travel. French doors led out into the garden.

More than just a place to live, for me the house symbolized a place of contentment, of calm, love and security where we would experience happiness just eating breakfast, opening the doors when the sun shone, or sitting together when it was cold and bleak outside.

The house encouraged growth and development. And not being at home was also part of the image, because this house was the starting point for journeys. It was a springboard for my children to enter the big wide world and a place they could always return to.

So while I was sitting there as a broken man in the ruins of my life, in the deep hole of my existence, I created a first, idealized image of my future. The future of myself and my family, of my dream house and my financial freedom in happier circumstances.

And by imagining it again and again, I anchored this future in my mind.

My visualization of the house turned out to be more than an imaginary journey, more than a daydream. Because you have daydreams without a specific context and without linking them to a conviction.

Daydreaming is more like a mild form of planning. Holiday time soon. You imagine what things you'll do when, how you will get ready and set off. It is a familiar kind of imagining, and is a form of looking forward to something. For many people, I have discovered, it's actually one of the best parts of the holiday.

A daydream about 'sometime later' is less accessible, linked to more preconditions and is sometimes frustrating. Then you dream about, let's say, a round-the-world trip, one day, when work and family will permit. After your retirement perhaps? A nice dream, but not much chance it will come true. Certainly less chance than realizing your normal holiday plans. This is due to the longer time between desire and fulfilment. Or maybe because a daydream serves no other purpose than giving everyday life a more attractive perspective?

But it's something else again when you make your distant daydream, such as a round-the-world trip, into a project. You start planning the world tour, because it's something you really want. In five years' time, maybe? Or three? There's a pretty good chance it will work out, as long as you have the conviction and you take the concrete steps, large and small, for making the dream into reality.

The striking thing is that the imagination, the daydream, can be a powerful instrument although in many cases you're not aware of it. Did you know you can use your imagination strictly to your advantage? All day long you imagine all kinds of things about everybody, including yourself, and this imagining determines your reality. Again, in most cases you're not even aware that you're imagining things. How do you mean, imagining? It's reality. I can see it with my own eyes, can't I? If you're in a foul mood, then the people around you are annoying and unpleasant. If you're happy, then all the world smiles at you. In love? Your partner is amazing! Getting divorced? What a bitch!

You see reality with your own eyes and interpret it in your own way. The world is good or bad, the future is dark or rosy, and the glass is half full or half empty, not to mention the bottle, too. Thanks to my rediscovered gratitude and the hope that followed on from this, I not only dared to turn my gaze cautiously toward the world once more but even, there in the Buddhist centre, to envisage an ideal future.

More intense and more comprehensive than a planned world tour, the imagining of my ideal future took the form of a symbolic house.

I saw the house from outside and from the inside. I saw myself in the mirror and experienced the emotions created by walking through the rooms of the house as its proud owner. So the image in my mind involved all my senses. This sense-related aspect can be different for each person, and have a different kind of persuasiveness. For instance, I can imagine that a musician would be able to hear his creation, and the cook to taste his. What does it look like, how does it feel, sound, taste and smell? Together the senses form an image in your mind that is as clear as the reality around you. What's more, while the image inside your head takes shape the reality around you fades and moves to the background of your perception. Now all your senses are focused on the experience of the image. Imagination pushes aside reality.

And mine was a reality I was only too happy to push aside. In contrast to my image of my ideal future as symbolized by the house there was another image: an unchanging future perspective. The situation I was in now was full of woe. What would happen if I kept doing the same things, if I stayed who I was? What if my future were to be an extension of the events I experienced, as it had been in the past? Just imagine, in five years from now. Or in ten, twenty years... Would I still be squatting in the ruins, still down in the hole? Would I be feeling four times worse by then?

Even the prospect of five years of the same was a frightening vision. Because five years on from that point would mean no house and almost no income. I could look forward to plenty of pain and few pleasant moments. My skin would be one big rash, because that's what I get when I'm stressed out.

But, I asked myself in the euphoria of my imagining, now that I had seen a little spark of hope in that intense mental image, why couldn't my future be ideal and wonderful instead of desperate and disastrous? After the revelation of my gratitude I had sensed my responsibility for the situation I had arrived at. And who else was responsible for my future but myself? Of course, I could fail in a new attempt to give my life better prospects, but doing nothing would mean failure anyway. And besides, I had already failed so monumentally that this factor hardly mattered. OK, there were plenty of problems and challenges. Change was difficult, threatening and scary but the alternative – where will I be in five years if I do nothing? – was dreadful.

Do you remember the example of the long-lost daughter who had been found 300 kilometres away? She served as an image for indicating the power of motivation: having a why.

What was even more powerful for me than this imaginary daughter was the expectation of the pain contained in an unchanged future, which drove me not only to imagine a new reality but above all to escape the present one. It was the strongest incentive I could imagine. This reason why I wanted to attain a new reality determined the strength I could apply to the mission.

Here's my message: your imagination is a powerful instrument. You start creating your future in your mind. Why not make your future and your perception of your current life more rosy? If you do that, are you closing your eyes to hard reality or is it a way of seeing reality with different eyes? I believe it's the latter, of course.

If you perceive or imagine something so intensely that it's already an incontrovertible reality in your head – a house, a future – then, and only then can you take the steps and possibly also the risks to realize this image in the physical world, too. But of course to do this you need to have and maintain the right motivation.

And what if reality doesn't seem to develop in line with your dream? How do you keep yourself on track then? By realizing that the doubts are real and that not everything is going to succeed. By adjusting the image, without abandoning it or constantly calling it into doubt. You realize your dream. If it doesn't work out, then you try again. There's no such thing as failure. And be aware that the image of the ideal will keep evolving, even if it's a house. It's a once-in-a-lifetime experience to feel how the imagination works, but it's not limited to a once-in-a-lifetime session.

14

Change, now

In his outstanding book The Seven Habits Of Highly Effective People, Stephen Covey sets out an approach to life in which you take responsibility for your own life and shape it to your own concept. He teaches us how we can improve the quality of our working life, private life and family life.

The quality of my life could certainly do with some improvement at that point. The gap between my reality and my dream was enormous. I had absolutely nothing, so how could I even start working on my imagined ideal? The dream house I had built in my head had been created without financial constraints, economic realities, advice from other people or day-to-day problems. But after the dream I awoke and all the obstacles were back in place again. How could I overcome these obstacles and keep hold of my dream?

Stephen Covey illustrates one of his insights with the circle of involvement and the circle of influence. The circle of influence contains the things we can change. The circle of involvement relates to things that concern us but which we cannot influence. Covey advises you to focus on the circle of influence. Let the rest be, because however much energy and trouble you devote to it, this won't change anything.

My circle of involvement had vaporized. I was past the point of getting angry about the supposed injustice I had suffered. My circle of influence seemed limited. If I was to set course for a new reality, I had to change something. But what? And how?

The only thing I could change was myself.

It had become clear that I had no influence whatsoever on all the other things. But how could I change myself? How long would this change take and, if it happened, when would it influence my situation? In five years? In ten, or fifteen? I couldn't wait that long, that would simply make my vision of the future too bleak. The only option I saw was to change the things I did and thought right now. Because my actions and my thoughts were the only things inside my circle of influence.

Luckily, science backs me up. Everything changes, even DNA, the building block of life. The phenomenon of DNA reprogramming lies within the field of epigenetics, and that's not something I know much about. But I have read a book on the subject: The Second Code by Peter Spork. He explains that you don't need a nuclear disaster to trigger changes in DNA. Going out for an energetic run is sufficient, because as soon as you physically exercise this affects the DNA in your muscles so that they can prepare for even higher performance. (It has to do with methyl groups, histones and RNA, writes Spork.) Major changes begin with small steps, so these were what I had to take. And besides this, I thought to myself, if the building block of life itself is so changeable, what certainties do we actually have? In fact, only the certainties you give yourself.

If you walk through the jungle for years, then a path will take shape along your route. If you want a new path, then you have to create it yourself. It's the same with thoughts and convictions. Over the years you produce them in countless numbers, and not achieving a goal is often reason enough to assume that you're no good, and you stop trying. If you want to change your convictions then it seems the neurons in your head need to create new connections with each other. So how do you go about it?

By changing your actions and thoughts now. The big ones and the small ones. I already mentioned Leo Bormans and the corners of your mouth. Lift them up and negative thoughts are blocked out. Chest out, shoulders back, chin up, and your attitude to the world regains strength. These are just a few examples of direct changes in attitude and behaviour. Thoughts too can be influenced immediately in this way. It begins with words.

Words are emotionally charged symbols. Just like the imagination, they form a powerful motivator and a dangerous instrument at the same time. You can use them positively or turn them against yourself and others.

Using words such as 'old', 'dull' and 'heavy' will create a corresponding feeling. Actions and thoughts will become older, duller and heavier. Words such as 'energetic', 'enthusiastic' and 'motivated' create a very different mood. They make you energetic, enthusiastic and motivated. Words and deeds are linked together. All you need to do is imitate an energetic, enthusiastic and motivated person. Do this and it will seem to be without words, but because this is a conscious imitating action you do actually form the words in your mind. There's nothing stronger than the combination of the spoken word and accompanying behaviour.

Just as my behaviour obviously hadn't been helpful for my ultimate well-being, so my words too had played their part, and here chiefly at the unconscious and unspoken level. My life, expressed in twelve words, was pretty much as follows:

Must.

Want.

Love.

Escape.

Adventure.

House.

Children.

Ambition.

Money.

Success.

Fear.

Failure.

I don't want to fail. I don't want to fail. I don't want to fail. The sound of that last word will take root. Fail, fail, fail. The word will come true. Nor for any mystical kind of reason, but because that one word in 'don't want to fail' forms the foundation for thoughts and deeds. It influences, it limits and it determines.

At the low point of my life and the climax of my disappointment, I charged up this word 'fail' with my own experience and applied it to myself. Fail is a word like any other. But you yourself give meaning and power to the words, and behind each word is a world of feelings to which you react. Words create images in your head and feelings in your heart.

So change it.

Avoid certain words in the same way you avoid irritating people. By doing so you not only give the word no chance to contaminate your thoughts – it also strengthens your self-discipline and your conscious-ness. Remove the negative charge from words you originally lent to them yourself, for instance by turning up the corners of your mouth while you speak them.

By communicating with yourself you stimulate yourself to actions and thoughts. You can motivate and inspire yourself, and lend power to each word spoken by you and to you. Make sure to use the 'good' words and avoid the 'bad' ones. Cultivate an energetic, enthusiastic and motivated spirit!

So there I was: my old certainties had disappeared. Why not create a new path through the jungle and discover and develop myself anew? But to achieve this I first had to gather up the fragments of my old life – study them, decide what to throw away or to keep. Which deeds and thoughts had formed my character? Who was I and above all: who did I want to become? I wanted to change my DNA and become a new Aqil.

15

Nobody sees the invisible man

There had been a phase in which I had attributed my ruin as an entrepreneur to vague phenomena such as the economic crisis, the unfairness of life or my own general lack of ability. This was now over. The reasons for my failure had to lie in a series of concrete, identifiable factors. A careful dissection of my 'failure' might, if I discovered the mistakes, give me the recipe for success. After all, do right what you did wrong before and things will work out OK. But I hadn't yet reached the stage where I could think in terms of success. What I did try to do was to explain the events in my recent past in order to alleviate my sense of powerlessness – no more than that.

As it turned out, it wasn't difficult to find concrete reasons for my failure. Practical experience had already demonstrated these facts to me, and indeed thoroughly rubbed my nose in it. A faulty personnel policy, for instance, in which I appointed my best technician as salesman and had the bookkeeping done by the wife of one of my employees. Or poor financial administration in general, for which I could blame no-one but myself. Figures were wrong, invoices floated all over the place, and all because I didn't wish to see myself as a shopkeeper but instead as a big-time entrepreneur. A third concrete and important factor in my failure was my shambolic order acquisition. To give one example, for a long time I had a list of potential clients to call, in front of me on my desk. But I didn't call them. Precisely at a time when I needed to build my turnover, I felt paralysed. I'm a damn good salesman, I know for sure. And nonetheless I didn't sell. Although I had a list of telephone numbers and names of companies and people, right there in my office, I didn't pick up the phone, even when I had a warm lead and there was a very good chance the potential customer could use our services.

Why?

This question was like a spade going into the soil, uncovering ever deeper layers of dirt to reveal the true reasons.

Why?

Because I was too lazy.

This seemed to be a good conclusion. It fitted the memories I had of myself in that period of looming bankruptcy. Lazy, reluctant, with other things on my mind.

Why was I lazy?

Simple. If you're lazy by nature, then it's logical that you won't get any acquisitions off the ground, right?

But... I'm not at all lazy by nature, am I? The call list may have remained untouched on my desk, but in the meantime I did lots of other things. Actually, I think I'm a very energetic person!

The spade pushed in deeper.

In one of the books I was to read, there was a very simple exercise which I reproduce here in my own words.

Select one action or undertaking which you know would make your life better, more enjoyable, happier, richer or healthier if you were to do it and succeed in it.

Have you got something?

Now write down the reason why you don't do it. (Don't think about it for too long, just what you always say to yourself and others, or the first reason that comes into your head.)

Now draw a thick line through this reason and underneath write in big letters 'BULLSHIT!'

You see, it's just an excuse that you deceiving yourself with. Or at least that's what I discovered when I did this exercise.

I wrote:

Action: Call customers and score contracts!

Reason why I don't do it: Laziness

BULLSHIT!

OK then, but what was the real reason?

I had another think.

The spade hit the bottom layer.

The reason that then came to light was to trigger a complete turnaround in my life. It would change the way I thought, perceived and acted. Its influence on me, my life and my future would prove to be overwhelming.

All those years I had been fooling myself and others! Me, Aqil Radjab, the great entrepreneur, the smooth talker, the easy-going guy, the big dude with his cheerful ego, was a completely different person than I had been pretending to be all my life.

Why?

I was quite simply afraid of rejection! And that was the reason why I was secretly happy to leave that list untouched on my desk, because it was full of 'maybes' that might mean my salvation. As long as the list was there, there was hope. As soon as I started calling, I could find myself crossing out the hope, number for number.

My inner monologue was something like this: 'If I have a warm lead, then at least I have a 'maybe'. If I call, then there's a chance I'll get a 'no' and that idea scares me so much... Not call? If I don't call, then nothing will ever come of it, so I might as well pick up the phone... No, I'll wait a little longer.'

The flash of self-insight was incredible. So incredible that, indeed, I didn't want to believe it. So my laziness was an excuse to keep me from facing the real reason, my fear of rejection? How unbelievable was that? Did I see a frightened man when I looked in the mirror? No, of course not. It was a load of nonsense.

But the truth was right there in front of me. I saw it and I knew it was undeniable. I, Aqil, was fearful and vulnerable. It wasn't exactly a conclusion to be proud of, but it was time to finally face up to it.

And so I did.

Finally.

After seven days.

It was so hard for me to accept this new picture of myself that I also saw it would have been impossible to gain the insight if events hadn't forced me to that point.

My understanding of the true reason changed the way I thought and the way I behaved. Now that I knew that fear lay behind my supposed laziness and behind my excuses and arguments, I asked myself how I could overcome it. I had no idea, although I was relieved that I was no longer on the wrong track. I could have continued to use the argument of my laziness, trying to force myself to overcome it, and then when I failed I could once again have excused myself with this laziness. Whatever conclusion I would ultimately have drawn, it would have been wrong because it was based on the wrong perspective.

But my fear of rejection had now come to the surface, undeniably, and in doing so had lost its hidden power. Now I understood what influenced me and held me back, and I could choose whether I wished to let it direct my actions or not.

And it also immediately answered the question I had put to myself. I didn't need to conquer the fear, to repress it or to shout it down. Recognizing it, acknowledging it turned out to be enough.

Nowadays if I have a list on my desk, I usually call the numbers right away. Not because I must, but because I enjoy doing it, and because I know that I genuinely have something to offer. Seven out of ten times I'm successful. And from time to time I still find it difficult to call, but then I realize the true reason and I can convince myself that I won't gain anything at all by not calling.

What's more, I've got a secret weapon for emergencies.

One of the most powerful sentences I know is something I read when I was aged around twelve. My mother had a subscription to Readers Digest. At the bottom of a page or article they often printed a one-liner. The sentence that really hit me was: "Nobody sees the invisible man".

When I feel afraid of rejection, for instance when I pick up the phone to make a call, I say this sentence out loud. The only person I say it to is myself. And if possible I say it aloud to myself while looking in the mirror: 'Nobody sees the invisible man.'

16

Shame on me!

I felt a terrible sense of shame during my bankruptcy, like a concrete block sitting in my guts, and as a consequence I didn't dare to hold my head high or to begin a dialogue with myself. It was a feeling of guilt that blanketed everything and prevented me from taking action, because as soon as an idea came into my mind I felt ashamed and abandoned it.

Shame is not a harmful emotion in itself, of course. Just like fear it stops you doing things you'll regret later. Shame also ensures that if you happen to fly off the handle, you quickly offer sincere apologies to those who you have hurt and thus enables you to restore the relationship. The question is whether the shame you feel is justified or whether the feeling is keeping you back unnecessarily. After all, shame is often the result of your assumptions about how those around you will react to something you have done or said. These assumptions are learned, and so you can unlearn them too. However, if you feel the shame is justified then you'll need to find a way to live with it and to park it, temporarily or permanently, in a place where it doesn't get in your way.

That's what I tried to do. It was incredibly difficult. I felt so horribly ashamed about not having the money to maintain myself and my family! And I was so ashamed that I had squandered the money borrowed from friends and family!

It was only after deciding for myself to park the feeling of shame that I was able to start building my new sense of self. And much later, when the 'construction work' had progressed far enough that I had some money on my hands again, I deliberately retrieved the feeling of shame and had conversations with everyone whom I had harmed in financial terms. From that moment on shame made way for gratitude and pride, because I was finally able to pay the money back to my friends and family, and ultimately with a good interest rate to top it off. By the way, the category of 'family' also included my sons, whose savings accounts had been included by the administrator in the bankruptcy assets at the time.

So I didn't cast off the shame – I acknowledged it. No, I'm still not proud of having wasted part of my youth, but nowadays I no longer find it so terrible. And no, I'm certainly not proud that I was a bad entrepreneur while also bearing responsibility for my family and my employees. But that's how it was. Since acknowledging it, I no longer carry the weight on my shoulders.

And I realized another thing too: if there's something you feel ashamed of, bring it into the open. This freely chosen vulnerability makes life easier and better, and it increases your chances of success.

'SET YOUR GOALS. DEFINE YOUR AIMS. WITHOUT AIMS LIFE IS... AIMLESS. IMAGINE THEM, FEEL THEM, WITH NO LIMITATIONS. REALITY WILL IMPOSE THE LIMITATIONS BY ITSELF, SO NO NEED TO WORRY ABOUT THAT. AND OF COURSE: DON'T BE AFRAID OF FAILURE, BECAUSE THERE'S NO SUCH THING. YOU MIGHT GET FRUSTRATING OR ANNOYING RESULTS BUT THESE TOO CONTAIN SOMETHING NEW AND VALUABLE. THE ONLY FAILURE IS NOT DOING WHAT YOU *WANT*.'

17

Self-development time

The Seven Habits of Highly Effective People wasn't the only book I read, of course. I wanted to improve myself and enrich myself mentally, I wanted to arm and armour myself. I was beginning to put the hardest times behind me, but I didn't want the experience to be in vain. So I learned, I processed and I came to terms. And this gave me the feeling I had a lifetime to catch up on, or years at least, which gave me a thirst for new knowledge.

Anthony Robbins taught me to evaluate my own behaviour critically and to set goals. Over the years I was to attend three presentations given by Robbins. The first of his seminars that I visited was in London. The trip cost me 700 euros which I scraped together from the debt restructuring programme. During breakfast I stuffed my bag full of bread so that I'd have something to eat during the day. I sat right at the back of the hall, but I was so eager to learn that I felt I was in the front row.

And since it was self-development time I bought books about transcendental meditation, heart coherence and family constellations. The Seven Habits of Highly Effective People, Simplify Your Life, Unlimited

Power... I travelled from The Hague to Rome and from London to New York to see and hear lectures by the best in the field. I learned from Richard Branson, Deepak Chopra, Stephen Covey, Anthony Robbins, Wim Sondagh, Ben Tiggelaar....

Not everything I learned was spiritual, revolutionary or enlightening. I learned, for instance, that I shouldn't let paperwork build up on my desk, but should put it in filing trays or boxes instead. If something takes less than thirty seconds to do, then do it right away. Pretty obvious, right? Well, not to me.

The seminars and the books taught me something new and important: how to view myself, my life and my environment in a critical and open-minded way. Not judgementally, not uncritically affirming and without any limiting preconceptions. And one of the most important lessons I learned was about my need for certainties.

Apparent certainties, self-confidence and judgements are formed to a great extent by our experiences, our environment and the people around us. Even while still in the womb we are influenced by tastes, sounds and moods. These early memories influence body and mind. They form your character and your thought patterns which will help to decide how you approach life. Do you get angry quickly, do you give up quickly, are you capable of love, are you eager to learn?

On the basis of this character, these thought patterns, your role models and preferences in your early life, you then form an image of yourself, the world around you and your position in it.

Can you name something in your life which would lead you to regard yourself as happy and successful, but this vision doesn't fit in with who you are now, how you live or how you experience the world?

Then change.

But that's easier said than done!
Yes, of course.
So how do you do it?
By being aware.

What was I actually happy or unhappy with? What things did I want to change? What was important to me? My health, my wife, children and other family, my friends, my business contacts, my finances, my career...

One thing I had learned to do was draw a wheel, with one of these life aspects at the end of each spoke. From the axle to the rim, each spoke had a score from 0 to 10. What score did I give myself for each of these aspects? I scored an 8 for family, a 6 for health, a 2 for finances and so on.

And the result was interesting: however lousy I might feel, I gave myself a pretty good score for just about all the essential aspects of my life. But I scored poorly on one point: my finances. And that one point negated all the others. It impaired my health and it detracted from my general sense of happiness.

But just by realizing that, I felt this negative influence decrease. After all, it seemed I had plenty of reasons for feeling gratitude in the other essential areas of my life. So I could put the financial situation in a new perspective: the perspective of the wheel, which by now looked more like a spider's web because the spokes were linked up by lines. And now that I understood that just one aspect was negating all the others, I was able to take a more mindful approach to the quality of my life. Not mope about when I was with Sascha and the kids, but instead enjoy their company and make the most of the moment.

Wow, what a discovery! Now I was even more determined to change my actions and thoughts. This option definitely lay within my circle of influence. The dream house was far away, my financial situation was bad, but there were so many things I could work on...

My wife, my children and other family members, my friends: I felt so thankful when I realized that I still had them, and that our relationships were good. Just as I had imagined my dream house in an intense way, so I now sensed in a similar manner how happy and grateful I was for this realization. I sat down, opened myself up to this feeling and thought about them until tears came to my eyes.

And then?

Then I picked up the phone and made some calls. I wanted to tell them. They had to know. I put my feelings into action.

And the result? The gratitude grew in me and took root. Happiness became part of me again, and I began to emanate it.

I'm not a Buddhist, but what I have understood is that there's a form of meditation in which you evoke peace and love for yourself and others. That's what I did, in my own way.

Everyone experiences pain. This, expressed in other words, is the First Noble Truth of Buddhism. Although I was starting to see family, health and finances from a new perspective, I still struggled with the pain that was within me and which I couldn't simply deny. I had to deal with this, too. I needed the courage to feel this pain. That pitiful score had to rise. Not from a 2 to a 9, because that was impossible and moreover unnecessary. But first of all to a 3 or a 4, in small steps, thus allowing the important elements in my life to achieve a better balance. But looking at the pain in this way I was able, as with the fear, to soften it to a degree.

Whatever I learned, from Buddha or Ben, the essence turned out *to be pretty much comparable, universal and worth repeating: you create an image of yourself and the world around you in your head. This image determines your role and your possibilities. It determines convictions and your limitations. Everything, but truly everything, is conceptualization. Just as you were able to create this image and to live accordingly, so you are also able to change it. After all, everything changes, even your DNA after going out for a good run. Or your mood after you decide to laugh. Or your motivation after you lift up your head and pull back your shoulders.*

And there's another essential thing I learned: there's no such thing as failure , only results. In the words of the writer and poet Samuel Beckett: 'Ever tried. Ever failed. No matter. Try again. Fail again. Fail better.' So get moving and set your goals!

18

Cheque!

At the time I wrote out these cheques, in early 2006, I was still in the debt restructuring programme. In financial terms I was still in the basement and had difficulty making ends meet. I wrote out five cheques, one for each year. And each cheque bore an increasingly extravagant amount, certainly considering my situation at the time. The first year's cheque was for a sum of 100,000 dollars, the second was for 160,000 dollars, the third for 250,000 dollars, the fourth for 400,000 dollars and the cheque for the fifth and final year was for 700,000 dollars. The amounts were in dollars because these were the only cheques I could find on the Internet.

I printed out the cheques, filled in the amounts and stuck them on the wall over my desk, in the attic of our little rented house. (I took them down again when we were moving house, and the corner of 2009 got torn off.)

I looked at the cheques almost every day. Not because I was obsessed with money and wanted to keep dollar signs in my eyes by staring at them, but because the cheques were my tickets to a more attractive destination. They were printed off the Internet, filled out by myself, were actually worthless – but they meant everything.

UNIVERSAL BANK (UN)LIMITED
DATE 31/12/2007
REMITTANCE ADVICE - Feel Good
PAY
$ 100,000.00
TO THE ORDER OF
One hundred thousand
DOLLARS
DRAWER: THE UNIVERSE ACCOUNT: UNLIMITED ABUNDANCE
SIGNED
This is not an instrument subject to Article 3 of the UCC
⑆843 732738⑆ 843 732738

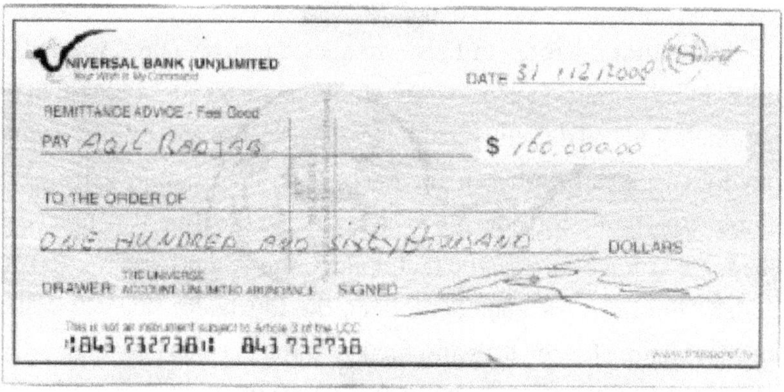
UNIVERSAL BANK (UN)LIMITED
DATE 31/12/2008
REMITTANCE ADVICE - Feel Good
PAY
$ 160,000.00
TO THE ORDER OF
ONE HUNDRED AND sixty thousand
DOLLARS
DRAWER: THE UNIVERSE ACCOUNT: UNLIMITED ABUNDANCE
SIGNED
This is not an instrument subject to Article 3 of the UCC
⑆843 732738⑆ 843 732738

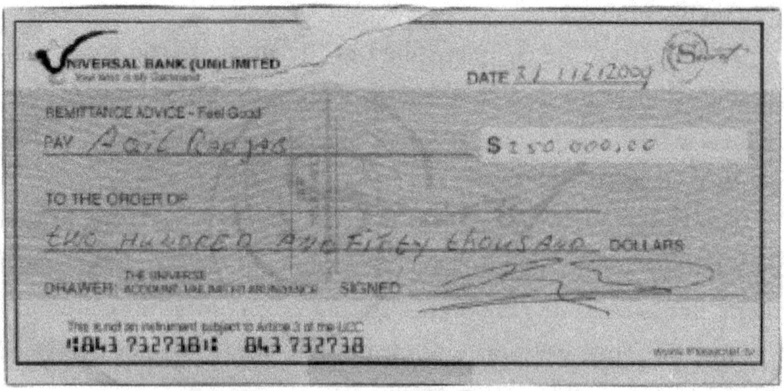
UNIVERSAL BANK (UN)LIMITED
DATE 31/12/2009
REMITTANCE ADVICE - Feel Good
PAY
$ 250,000.00
TO THE ORDER OF
two HUNDRED AND FIFTY thousAND
DOLLARS
DRAWER: THE UNIVERSE ACCOUNT: UNLIMITED ABUNDANCE
SIGNED
This is not an instrument subject to Article 3 of the UCC
⑆843 732738⑆ 843 732738

In both the book and the film The Secret by Rhonda Byrne it's said that something will happen if your desire for it to happen is really strong enough. But I don't believe it will unless you take action as well. If I want to blow out a candle, then just sitting there wanting and waiting won't achieve much, will it? You have to do the blowing yourself. As regards myself and my situation, I wanted to take action. And because I was so convinced that I would realize my dream, I realized that the how would reveal itself, too. Because if the how didn't come, how could I then be convinced?

I knew what I wanted in broad terms: I had convinced myself that it was definitely going to work out, but I hadn't yet discovered how. In my mind I already had the image of my dream house, a sense of change and wisdom from others that I had made my own. Now I wanted to make them reality and for this I needed goals and a point of reference. This was what the cheques gave me.

I also knew I had to be able to learn from my mistakes. And that by learning I could ensure I wouldn't make the same mistakes again. And that I could be responsible for success. This success would be the reward for the difficult but instructive years I had been through. Moreover, I could see the reward ahead of me, namely the house, the amounts on the cheques and above all the life I could lead in connection with these things. A dream life that I aimed to make reality.

By now, thanks to those two little white socks, I was a grateful and happy person. But if you're grateful and happy, then why still strive for something else? After all, without a goal your happiness is a state of being that belongs to the present moment, and that's undeniably Zen.

True, but I'm not Zen, I'm Aqil. I can be intensely happy with

The checks with the desired income.

what I have and with who I am, but in my character there's always something that wants to move towards the future. I have dreams and ambitions, and if I don't translate these into goals then I feel restless and dissatisfied. I've tried it, of course. As soon as I had found my happiness I thought: right, from now I'll just be nice and 'Zen'. But it didn't work out. I could be happy for a little while in this way but I soon started to get the itch. What I really needed was a goal I could work towards with commitment, because that enriches my life. I get a huge amount of energy and joy from travelling the path to these goals. There are challenges, there are setbacks, but these can never be so big as to hold me back. Remember, there's no such thing as failure , only results, and they may be disappointing. Everything needs to grow, and stasis leads to unhappiness. In order to grow we need goals. But nonetheless, you should never make your happiness and sense of gratitude dependent on the goals you wish to achieve in the future. I know that, because I was unhappy.

How did I know what direction to take? By considering what makes me happy and joyful, and choosing the route that takes me there. I chose the route by fixing a grand, compelling point on the horizon and then defining the feasible goals that would get me there.

19

Five hundred euros

I started applying for jobs. I did this by writing letters, and when I didn't write letters I made phone calls instead. I must have sent out around twenty applications a day. And I only applied to listed companies because I wanted to be sure that my potential employer would pay me and that the company wouldn't go bust the way mine had. The past years had made me wary and distrustful in this area, too.

I was invited to interviews. To go to one of these interviews, which took place in a hotel, I borrowed a friend's car. My own car had been repossessed. I calculated that the petrol would cost me fifteen euros. At the start of the interview we ordered coffee. In order to make a good impression I paid for it. After the interview I had to exit from the car-park but got stuck at the barrier. The parking charge was fifty cents and I didn't have it. I had to go back to the hotel to borrow money.

I wrote good letters, I showed an enthusiastic attitude and I behaved the right way. So why did all these interviews come to nothing?

Due to a simple error of reasoning. Not wanting to take any risks I applied only to listed companies. But listed companies didn't want to take any risks either. As soon as I mentioned in the concluding part of the interview that I was in a debt restructuring programme, my fate was sealed.

After months of fruitless job applications, I decided to remain silent about my bankruptcy and its consequences.

The very next interview proved a success. I was accepted as a branch manager for a large temping agency. It was only at the moment that they wanted to pay my salary that I told them the money had to go to an administrator. My employer gave me the benefit of the doubt and let me stay on. And that's something for which I'm still hugely grateful.

The regular work and routines at my new employer gave me a sense of calm and security – which was something enormously important to me at that time. But how could I improve the situation for myself and above all for my family? Because however well I earned, all the money went to the administrator. The four of us still had to live on 1100 euros a month. And we had to pay the rent from that, too. After six months I received a large bonus but I had to hand that over as well. I couldn't buy shoes for my kids and my wife was walking round in old clothes. We didn't have a TV because we couldn't pay the bill. Was that so terrible? No. Was it a pain? Yes. And it was a constant reminder to me of my failure.

So I started doing some calculations.

Five hundred euros a month extra became my long-distance goal. For someone who couldn't even buy a cup of coffee or a carton of milk that was a big and seemingly unattainable sum. Nothing new for me in principle, because my dream house and the amounts on the cheques seemed just as unattainable. And so to make it feasible after all, I divided it into smaller sums. Every day I had to earn a little extra money: twenty euros. So I started doing odd jobs for friends. If someone wanted me to hang up a new picture frame for them, once I'd finished I asked what they wanted to do with the old one. And then I sold it for five euros through an online marketplace.

I was still in survival mode, but I consoled myself with the thought that by now I had enough to eat and a roof over my head. No, more than that. I had a job and was earning just a little extra on the side.

And so I was increasingly able to count my blessings instead of my worries and insecurities. Every morning. My employee status provided me with a foundation of calm and security. And once again, part of my self-assurance was restored as soon as I found I was able to meet my family's primary needs: with the five hundred euros a month.

These were small mental and practical steps towards my great dream.

20

Setting goals

When I founded my first company I set myself lots of goals. I wanted to earn X amount of money and to do this I needed Y amount of people.

On the basis of who I was and what I knew at the time, that was only logical and sensible. That's how I had learned it, and that's how I did it. Moreover, it suited me fine. I believed that achieving a goal was the same as achieving happiness. What a wonderful feeling and what a great ego-boost! Look, there, on the horizon! That's where the railway tracks converge and that's where I need to be. Go, go, go! Wow, lots of adrenaline, so much motivation… All charged up and restless, I was fully focused on achieving my goal and proving I was right. And there was nothing wrong with that.

No, absolutely nothing.

Nothing at all.

Except…

Damn it, the goal was moving.

The point where the rails now converged was a horizon further on.

Luckily there were still a few landmarks here and there for me to get my bearings. A fixed point at the same place on the horizon that I'd now reached. I was now where I wanted to be, and felt pride and happiness with all I had achieved. But only for a moment. Then I had to move forward again, once again searching for the point on the horizon.

I was overlooking something.

It's not about the point on the horizon, it's about the way you look at it. If you stand between the rails and gaze at the distant point where they converge, then you can also imagine that over there, on the horizon, there's someone else gazing out as well. Maybe this person is looking your way and sees, in turn, the point where the rails converge. So what's the significance of these goals? And what's the use of achieving them?

Actually, it is useful. With a goal in my sights I knew what decisions I could make and I had a motive for action. My mistake was in assigning the goal too much absolute value, and in associating it with happiness. As soon as I achieve my goal, so my reasoning went, I'll be happy. No, you must be happy first – not happy later, subject to all kinds of conditions. The goal is a means to an end, nothing more. A goal can be expressed in terms of money, as I did in my new situation where the cheques served this purpose. But above all I wanted to be happy and my financial difficulties stood in the way of this.

What was I already happy with, and what did I want to change? The spokes of the wheel became my five goals and I arranged these in a certain order. And each time the question was: what I am doing now, and what's my goal for five years in the future?

1. Health. I could make impressive plans for every life area, but without the energy to carry them out they would be useless. So I had to improve and maintain my health.

2. Private life. My relationship with my wife and children was, and is, my top priority. They always were and are a huge part of my life, and they love me unconditionally. As I do them.

3. Other relationships. Friends and acquaintances are the first circle of happiness around the core of family.

4. Financial. Life is difficult if you don't have the money for it. So I wanted to create a perspective here.

5. Career. That's the thing most visible to the world in general, but for me it's the least important – although still important enough to formulate corresponding goals.

Later on I added another two goals to these five, which are still important to me today: giving back, or in other words helping people to be happy, and continuing to feel gratitude.

I devoted time to seated, focused meditations in which I pictured for myself what I wanted for each of my goals. All I did here, in peace and quiet and with no time pressure, was to imagine my possible future. To do this I shut out all disruptive influences and doubts and let my imagination flow free. Once again it was an escape from reality, a holiday spent in a dreamed future. It wasn't only an imaginary journey in unspoken words, but above all in images, sounds, sensations, smells: everything that can intensify an experience. I also wanted to feel the happiness I aimed to create for others, because that would inspire me to the deeds that were necessary to realize my dreams.

The goals I set myself seemed hard to achieve, and this was exactly why I made them real in my mind and thus reality for myself. If they remained too abstract they would not be credible. If I hadn't visualized my new house, then I would never have been able to build it. If I hadn't made the cheques and stuck them up above my desk, then I would never have taken the decisions that were necessary for gaining these amounts. Because I had set the goals, I was able to consider what I needed to do to achieve them. The goals on the dollar cheques were clear, but of course goals in real life keep changing. After all, your surroundings, the waters you sail on, are constantly changing, and as you make progress, so your goals shift and extend as well. But they continue to act as a beacon that guides you in the right direction.

Just as when imagining my house, I didn't consider physical, mental or financial limitations when setting my goals. I also left behind any limiting beliefs. Things like: I'm not good enough for that, or my wife won't allow it. What I wanted was a list of things I would really like to have if there were no limitations on time and space. If I had applied these limitations, then I wouldn't have got far. Take my entrepreneurial success, for instance. There had come a moment in my life when I no longer believed I was suited to be an entrepreneur. It was only after I had convinced myself that I really could learn the requisite entrepreneurial skills that I was able to continue and to imagine a successful future in this field. Up until then I was stuck in one place, reproaching myself for all kinds of things and envious of people who did achieve certain goals.

Naturally, some goals turned out to be more or less impractical. The important thing for me wasn't to achieve them, but to strive for them. That's because they form the point where the rails seem to converge, which means that they shift by themselves as you get close, and new goals then emerge to replace them. Removing boundaries and thus doubts and limitations ensures that the goals are pure. What's more, it's inspiring. Inspiration lets you achieve amazing things, and inspiration isn't helped by limiting beliefs.

You achieve goals by not stopping until you get there. It doesn't matter how you arrive there: by car, by train, on your bike or on foot.

Just keep going. But you'll encounter challenges on the path and you'll need to sacrifice some things to get where you want to be. Time, for instance. Or money and security. If the image of the goal you keep in your mind isn't strong enough and your heart isn't charged with all the good feelings associated with the goal, then many things on the path will feel like sacrifices to you. And that makes the path tough and the goal less easy to achieve.

Imagine that someone gives you a plant as a birthday present. The morning after your party you come downstairs, your eyes start to itch and your nose starts to run. Oh, it turns out you're allergic to the plant. So it has to go. Does this feel like a sacrifice? No, not at all, even though it's a pretty plant. But what happens if you love your cat and you find out you're allergic to this pet? If you get rid of your cat then it does feel like a sacrifice, but the same applies if you keep it, too. Because you keep sneezing and sniffing, and all because of that cat on your lap. Now let's make things a bit more extreme and suppose that the doctor says you're allergic to your own child. Will you throw him or her out of your house? No. You're happy to make the sacrifice and you keep loving your kid even as you sniff, sneeze and rub your eyes. The sacrifice is easy and indeed might not even feel like one, because it's about your own child, right? So what's the problem with itchy eyes and a runny nose in that case?

And that's how it is with a goal that you desire in your heart. Love it like a child, and no sacrifice is too great.

Imagining a goal, and then travelling the path towards this goal, is one of the finest activities in life for me. It's a journey that you can look forward to and where you form an image of what you'll see and experience long before you get there. In this way you live more than just once, and each of the experiences is intense.

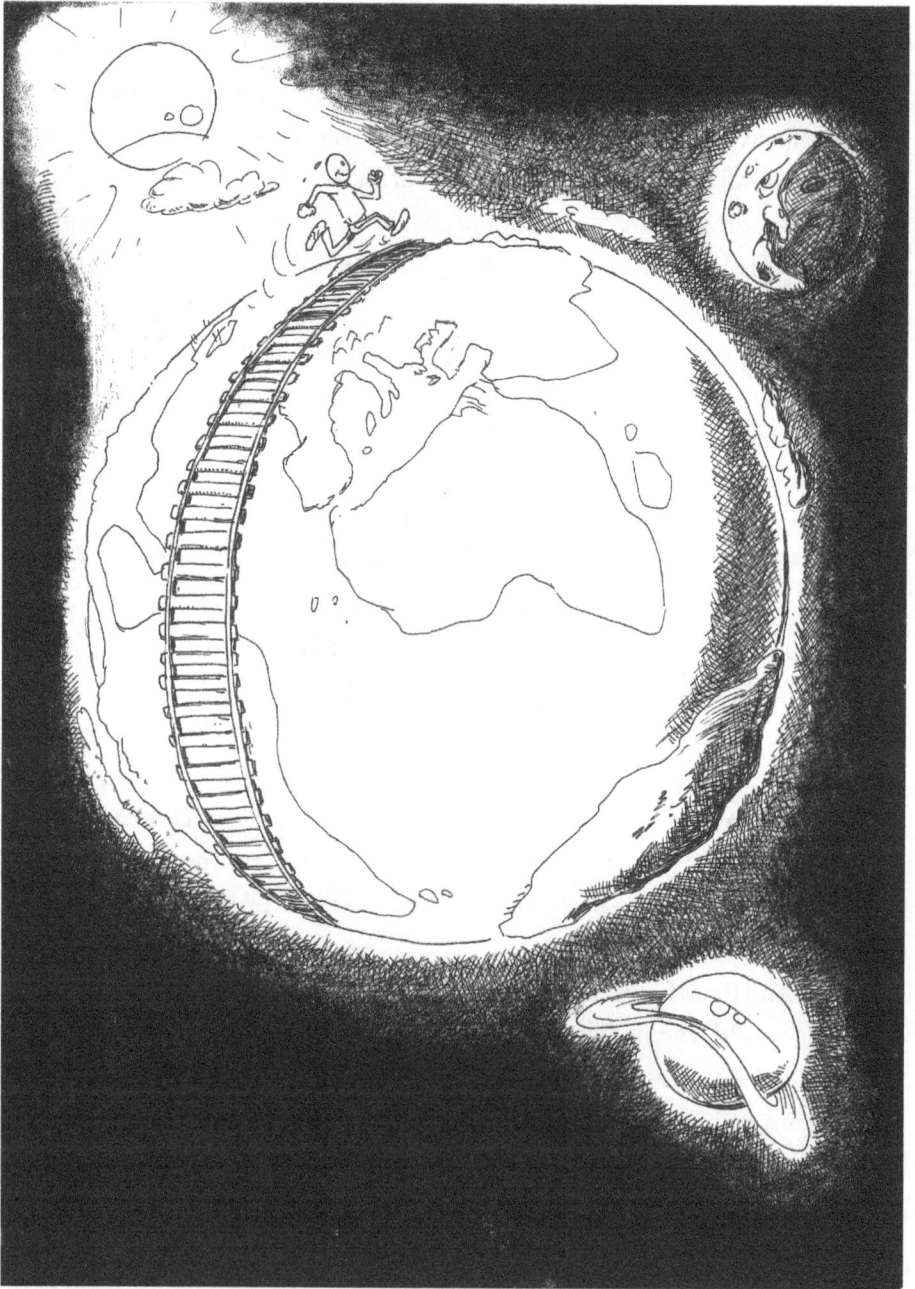

21

Casting the net

It was time for me to look the invisible man in the eyes. No more isolation, but instead time to meet people, build new relationships, make myself stronger and develop myself.

Networking!

At seven o'clock in the morning.

'Huh? Why so early?' I asked when I saw the invitation.

'What's the problem? Do you have anything else scheduled at that time? Seven in the morning – you've got no excuse not to come!'

That was true. It was hard to refuse the invitation. Even though I hadn't had many good experiences with networking in general, and with early mornings in particular.

In the period before my bankruptcy I had already been a member of a networking club. When an invitation to a meeting came, I turned up, drank coffee, shook a few hands and then wandered around feeling lost amidst two hundred other networkers focused on new business. I tried to score some contacts and deals but had little or no success due to the uncomfortable, forced atmosphere.

Would things be any different this time? Would I be any different?

The networking breakfast club was called BNI. It's an American formula with branches in various regions of the Netherlands. And there was one in my area, too, called BNI Dopper after a local director/composer.

As it turned out, I really enjoyed the early-morning meeting with around twenty other bigger and smaller entrepreneurs. I felt welcome at the breakfast table, where I sat down with entrepreneurs active in other areas to mine and found I could learn a lot from them.

I wanted to become a member, but a thousand euros a year was too much for me.

So I didn't join.

Then I did some sums.

Thought about it.

Hesitated.

And joined after all.

From that moment on my network mushroomed, because the weekly breakfast didn't mean a few sandwiches and a lot of hot air but instead provided structure, clarity, obligations and results. To begin with I wasn't so keen on the obligations but these taught me to fulfil my commitments even better. And at each meeting, in the early morning, we sat down with a full group of people.

After just two or three breakfasts I found myself surrounded by friendly ambassadors, each of whom had their own network. And as we got to know each other we learned to trust and help each other.

Aside from all the warm leads I suddenly had, something else proved to be equally or even more important: the personal development that the network triggered in me. I increasingly discovered that for me

BNI functioned as a training institute which got me moving again after years of standstill. How could I present myself and my product so that people would remember me? How could I introduce someone to my network and how could I myself get referrals? And above all, what does 'Givers Gain' really mean?

Givers Gain: not focusing on getting business but finding out how you can help someone else. Wow, that suited me so well! I took the things I learned at BNI and started applying them to other networking organizations. I made appointments, went to meet-up events and introduced my contacts to everyone's advantage.

The results were so astounding and made me so enthusiastic that, together with a good friend, I flew to England where we attended a BNI training programme. After that we started our own BNI region in the east of the Netherlands. It became the fastest-growing region in the world, rapidly acquiring hundreds of members.

And now? Many of my best friendships and business relations have emerged from BNI. And years after my first early breakfast, the company I was building at the time, Payroll Company, is still gaining millions of euros in turnover from the network.

Having breakfast with someone every week at seven in the morning creates a lifelong bond...

22

The right decision – not always easy

Joy van der Stel is a good friend of mine. She's married and has a daughter, Star. Joy is very successful in business and she's an author, too. In her book The Power of my Disability she recounts how she has been able to achieve her fantastic success and life. I suggest you buy and read the book because, believe me, Joy has achieved the incredible.

Due to a lack of oxygen Joy was born spastic. The doctor said something along the lines of: 'Don't write any birth announcements, because this one isn't going to make it.' They thought she was mentally handicapped as well and that the chances of any 'normal' life were pretty much zero.

But she made it.

There was nothing wrong with her mind – on the contrary.

If Joy had accepted what a doctor said right at the beginning, then indeed she wouldn't have made it. Then she wouldn't have had an education, wouldn't have taken up a profession, or had a relationship and a wonderful daughter. I've met Star: what a lovely, beautiful girl!

If Joy had listened to other people, the only thing she would have achieved would have been to prove them right and to confirm their view of reality instead of hers. Luckily she didn't listen to people who had a view of her future that she didn't share. They, the advising doctors, had limiting convictions and these weren't in line with hers. But she did listen to her parents. They taught her that she was responsible for her own life and that she shouldn't leave this to others. To doctors, for instance. So she accepted this responsibility and didn't give it up it again.

Joy is a special person and the example I give here is just as exceptional as she is. Because usually it's a good idea to put aside precisely the advice that comes from those who love you and want the best for you. Your parents, for instance. This is because their frame of reference is based on their own life, which you too form part of and which has achieved a certain balance. Changes to this balance mean disruption. What's more, they want to shield you from pain, disappointment and all the other hardships of a life where you choose an unfamiliar path. It's a loving intention that usually doesn't help you.

During my bankruptcy and when I found myself in the debt restructuring programme I often thought back to the letter my father had sent me in the last days of my career as seaman third class: 'don't do it.' I felt ashamed about leaving the navy despite his words, giving up my family's security and choosing the life of an entrepreneur. A disastrous path, as it had turned out. Had he been right to warn me? Should I have listened to him?

At the time the answer seemed clear to me. Everything pointed to him being correct, and what right to my own opinion did I still have? It took me a long time to recover and arrive at a new insight. Yes, his warning was justified. No, I was right in not listening to him.

Ultimately there's only one person who knows what you are capable of, and that's you. Maybe you make an error of judgement, but this decision will surely have a smaller error of margin than if someone else had made it for you, won't it? If the judgement or decision is wrong and you don't achieve the results you wanted, then it will probably help you to make a better decision next time and to achieve better results. As you continue on your path you learn more about yourself, your specialist field, your drive and your own truth. And who knows: maybe you can do infinitely more than what you thought you were capable of. You'll never discover this if you choose to limit your own process and development on the basis of other people's opinions.

It's essential to decide for yourself whose advice you follow and which things you ignore. Quite often the advice you get is based on a hierarchic relationship – from parent to child or from counsellor to someone seeking help. This makes it difficult to set aside the advice after considering it, all the more so because it can feel unnatural to disregard well-meaning and sincere advice from those who love you. And nonetheless, that's just what you need to do. Or at least for a while, long enough to answer the following question: is the advice in line with my own dreams and ambitions? And with the goals I associate with these? In the end it's not about what others say, but about what you then do with their words.

Just as it feels unnatural to disregard advice from those who are close to you and love you, so it also feels alien to distance yourself from those who confirm you in your identity at a certain moment in your life.

The little village to which I moved when I was fifteen seemed like the back of beyond to me. I came from the civilized west and landed in... well, where was I, then? On the street in any case, because there was no keeping me at home and at school. I surrounded myself with others who felt the same: young guys like me who liked to spend their time playing cards, smoking and drinking. Day and night, if possible. And so they confirmed me in what I thought I wanted and what I did – just like I did for them, I guess. But the things I thought and did weren't good for me. Sascha realized that. My parents too, but Sascha gave me a constructive alternative while my parents' advice came over as reproaches or accusations which I closed my mind to. And as soon as I moved to a new place with Sascha I escaped the sphere of influence of the friends whose company I liked so much.

You choose your natural friends on the basis of shared themes. These can be a vision of life, behaviour, music, clothes, or whatever. The choice is influenced by association, recognition, familiarity, confirmation... In fact these are all themes and qualities that confirm a status quo.

Apparently, it's not unusual in a job application process that the candidate selected as a new colleague is just a little less good than the person making the decision. Unconsciously (secretly?) it feels good to be the better person, also among your peers. Could it be the same in friendship? But if so, who will then serve as a role model for you?

If you dream of a seemingly unattainable house, write cheques for insane amounts and talk about goals that seem far out of reach, then most people say you are crazy. Not because you are, but because they think you are. I believe that on the one hand there are people who love you and want to protect you, but that on the other hand there are also people who find it threatening if you step outside an assumed reality. In comparison to their and your circumstances, your goals are disproportionate. But what's even more disproportionate is when you actually manage to achieve them. That gives everyone's sense of reality a jolt. Suddenly it seems that reality is a bit less reliable than assumed because someone else – Joy for instance, or me – escaped from it. This might give others a feeling of being left behind, which in turn prompts explanations like 'he or she got lucky'.

Lucky? I find it fascinating to understand where and how Joy drew strength from her disability. How did she manage, in her seemingly limiting circumstances, to set her goals, to pursue them and to achieve them? This question requires three answers, of which the first two are the most interesting. How are you able to set your goals, and then to pursue them? The third answer, how to achieve them, is actually a consequence of the first two. And because goals tend to shift, it's also the least important. What's more, the path towards the goals is the best part of the fun.

I've already described how I set the goals for myself. Now I'll tell you how I pursued and achieved them. And so I proudly present:

The Radjab Matrix ©

'ACTING ON THE BASIS OF INITIATIVE AND STRENGTH IS THE ONLY PROPER WAY TO ACHIEVE HAPPINESS AND SUCCESS.'

23

The Radjab Matrix ©

Neo: What is the Matrix?
Trinity: The answer is out there, Neo, and it's looking for you, and it will find you if you want it to.

I have been profoundly influenced by the books of Anthony Robbins and Stephen Covey. They inspired and taught me. Both Robbins and Covey write about the possibilities for taking action. The short version of this is: either you react to a situation, or you take the initiative.

	WEAK MIND	STRONG MIND
REACTIVE	Doubt/Denial (excuses)	Fight/short periods to avoid pain (forcing)
INITIATIVE	Escape	Determined/takes pleasure over the long term

The Radjab Matrix © is based on this and describes the combinations between state of mind and (re)action. Either you feel strong or you feel weak. Based on one of these two states of mind, you either react to events or you take the initiative yourself.

Do you remember my list of potential clients? The ones I was going to call... It lay on my desk for quite a while and I made little use of it. Why? To begin with I thought it was due to my laziness but self-scrutiny pointed to something more fundamental: the fear of being rejected. Sometimes I avoided the list, from time to time I looked at it, occasionally I even picked up the phone and at other moments I found new tasks that prevented me from calling or even coming near my office. Whatever I did, it was never based on initiative and strength. And so the potential clients on the list were hardly aware of my existence. I remained the invisible man.

The various combinations in the matrix contributed nothing to my success and very little to my happiness.

If I reacted on the basis of weakness then the result was doubt and denial. My doubt showed itself as the insecurity that prevented me from calling. My denial showed itself in the way I made up excuses for not touching the list and doing something else instead. I told myself I was lazy while in reality I was afraid of rejection. As long as I didn't call, I wouldn't hear a 'no' from a potential client and so in a twisted way I could still hope for a 'yes'. And I needed that hope because business was already so bad.

If I reacted to the list on the basis of strength, then I resolved to call the telephone numbers before ten o'clock in the morning. Then I walked to my office, but first found a few other things to do. Make coffee, shift some papers around... Then, at a quarter to ten, I started calling. Because I told myself: 'you must do it'. Maybe it brought some kind of result, but it wasn't really convincing. The call felt forced, half-hearted, there was no flow. And then I'd done it, finished. Until the next time, which again I put off for as long as I could. Just like a reaction based on weakness, my actions – or the lack of them – revolved unwillingly around the list on my desk. It was the list that influenced and determined events, not me.

I could also take the initiative, but then on the basis of weakness. In that case I made sure that I didn't even go near my office and the call list, and I gave priority to other things. I wasn't troubled by doubt or denial, because my initiative gave me the sense of doing things right. Unfortunately, I devoted lots of energy to the wrong things. I threw myself into tasks that didn't help me change the situation I found myself in. It was irrelevant time-wasting. And, above all, flight from the perceived threat.

The only good way of dealing with the list of potential clients would have been on the basis of initiative and strength. Then I would have approached the list full of enthusiasm because the names it contained could help me along on my path to happiness and success. When you act on the basis of initiative and strength many objections disappear by themselves. They no longer exist because you no longer see them. Or to put it better, because you no longer think of them. That's because every imaginable objection is, indeed, something you imagine yourself. It's a figment of the imagination. And because they no longer exist, you no longer need to devote attention to them or try to overcome them. You can focus on your goal instead of your objections.

So why didn't I do that? Fear held me back and whispered problems and excuses in my ear. And because I didn't realize where they were coming from, I treated them as objective and logical arguments.

One example of a self-created objection that can impede happiness and success is the common fallacy behind which I often hid: 'I don't have the time for it...' I used this excuse every hour, on the hour. Now, everyone has the same number of hours in the day, but I seemingly had less time than other people to do what I needed to do. And when I did it, I didn't do it well.

And why was this? For the same reason that applied to calling my potential clients.

Business was going badly, so in response I could decide to sit at home with my family, because there wasn't much work anyway. The consequence was that I neglected work and spent time at home, but in a tense and worried state. Or I would go to the office without achieving anything and I would hardly ever be at home.

Just like the rest of the world, I had 24 hours per day at my disposal, but I didn't put them to good use. And whatever I chose to do, it was always wasted time and effort. My timing was bad, I was inconsistent and weak-minded, my actions lacked integrity and conviction.

But what should I have done? How could I have used my time on the basis of initiative and strength?

By setting priorities. You choose one thing, and so you leave other things aside. And what do you choose? The thing that, on the basis of your own dream, goals and direction, will contribute to happiness and success.

Right now I'm choosing to write this book, while at the same time I'm experiencing difficult situations with both my mother and my wife. Both are ill. My mother terminally. It hurts not to be with my family. It's a choice. So why do I choose, at this moment and with full conviction and enjoyment, to write? Because I want to help people to be happy and I believe that what I write can contribute to this. And of course I want to be with my family too, so I arrange my time accordingly. Consciously, on the basis of initiative and strength.

My son recently asked me: 'Daddy, don't you enjoy being at home?'

I answered: 'I certainly do. But I enjoy the balance of working, being busy and being with you.' He understood me, even though he didn't necessarily like it. Am I too tough? One day he called me. He was in tears. 'Daddy, I miss you so much!' I cancelled all my appointments and took a mini-holiday with Tygo.

What do you choose to do with your time? The things that bring balance to the goals you have set yourself. And when it feels good – gives you joy and makes you happy – then you know you're doing the right thing. Your head supplies the rational aspects, your heart expresses emotions, but your gut will tell you the truth.

If you would like something in your life and it doesn't come about, then you can ask yourself why that's so. What happens to stop you realizing it? A lack of time, maybe? Every initial reason you give is wrong. Start by considering whether you want it enough and have set the right goals which are in balance with each other. Then if this is the case, see whether you are striving to achieve them on the basis of initiative and strength. Take a look at your own thoughts and behaviour. In which quadrant are you?

Only one of them is the right place to be.

24

Taking your chance

The path to happiness and success isn't actually that complicated. Steady as you go, as we say at sea. If you want to join the police in the future, for instance, you make sure that as a minimum you stay on the straight and narrow, act and think accordingly and acquire the necessary qualifications. You avoid getting sidetracked, distracted or involved in dubious stuff, and if you do decide on a little excursion then you ensure you get back on track afterwards.

And that's just how it works as soon as you decide to free yourself of the limitations from your past, if you want to own a house or to achieve independent financial status. If you want happiness and success, then set course towards your dreamed-of future. It's a path on which you can encounter and recognize people and opportunities that can help you directly and indirectly to achieve your new world. It's a path where you have the thoughts and make the choices that send you in the right direction.

Is it really that simple?

Yes, it really is that simple. It's not a self-fulfilling or self-fooling prophecy, it is – by definition – a self-fulfilled prophecy. What I mean here is that the prophecy is already true at the moment that it's made. Because if you dream about and believe in this future then this future already becomes part of your life. And right from the first moment on, this makes you happier than you were before. The path or direction you choose immediately leads you to true happiness and success.

And if things don't go as you expect? There's a Dutch singer/presenter called Gordon who is a great example of perseverance and entrepreneurial spirit. All his life he has been working on his career. Getting up at four in the morning to start work. He has been involved in all kinds of activities and not everything has been a big success, but he just keeps on going. Nowadays everyone says it's all just fallen into his lap, but this guy has worked his butt off to get where he is. That's an indispensable ingredient for happiness and success – although I couldn't tell you how happy Gordon is.

I found a formula on the Internet for calculating your chances of success in the lottery. Let chance 1 = Q (winning) and let chance 2 = K (5 correct numbers), let chance 3 = M (4 correct numbers), let chance 4 = F (3 correct numbers), let chance 5 = T (2 correct numbers), let chance 6 = C (1 correct number), let chance 7 = Y (0 correct numbers) and r = the possibility of having 1 of the 7 chances. A = the set of chances. And then you get:

$$A = \frac{Q + (\sqrt[r]{K} + M)T}{C - F}$$

I don't understand the formula, but I'm sure the result indicates that your chance of success in the lottery is not particularly great. And once you've bought a ticket, your opportunities for increasing this chance are zero. The best you can do is make sure you don't lose the ticket and look after it carefully, because otherwise you can wave goodbye to even this small chance of success.

What does 'a chance' mean for me? Certainly not a lottery ticket. In my view, a chance is an opportunity that presents itself and that leads you to success. The better prepared you are, the more often you see opportunities. Such chances present themselves every day, and you encounter the chance of a lifetime at least once every two weeks.

Seeing chances, opportunities, doesn't require eagle eyes but an open mind.

I remember the time that my wife Sascha was pregnant with our oldest son Emir. Wherever I looked: pregnant women, just like Sascha. Hmm, strange, because before this time they had hardly existed. Sure, I'd encountered one from time to time, a friend perhaps, whose face looked a bit rounder than usual, not to mention her belly, but that didn't happen too often. And now? Pregnant women all over the place! I saw them when visiting friends, on the street, in magazines and at home. And that wasn't all. A few months later, lots of mothers with prams and buggies appeared as well. Not to mention babies. Where in heaven's name did they all come from so suddenly? And why was I now bumping into them all?

And what goes for pregnant women goes for opportunities as well. As soon as you're tuned in to recognizing chances, then you see them everywhere. That doesn't mean you consciously or compulsively seek them, because you don't do that with pregnant women either. But you're on the right wavelength and so you see them as soon as they enter your field of vision. You're open to them in mental terms.

We have a dog at home, Sammie. My sons just love him. They think it's great when this pet sleeps in their beds. He feels the same way and – in his doggie way – regularly asks to do it. But sometimes they grab him and lay him down beside them. And then Sammie jumps off again. Why? For the same reason that love won't work out if you make the other person feel stifled. If you want to love someone, then you mustn't smother him or her; you must be able to let go, too. Grabbing, smothering, stifling... it all betrays an element of desperation or dependence. What do you do if you see a chance, or when an opportunity presents itself? You don't grab the chance, you embrace it. It's a game, something that gives you pleasure, and you play it in an easygoing and relaxed way, but on the basis of initiative and strength. That's flow.

It's easy for me to talk but that doesn't mean that everything went, or goes, easily for me. Because in order to be able to see and make use of opportunities, I first had to experience pain and failure as a person and as an entrepreneur. And of course, I didn't always manage to utilize my chances in an easygoing and relaxed way either. There are things that I got involved in which turned out differently than I had expected. I now understand the theory on the basis of practical experience. Which doesn't mean that I have, or will, always put theory into practice with equal success.

It's important to realize that what applies to opportunities also applies to setbacks. If you think and see in a negative way and if you believe in misfortune then you'll constantly find this confirmed, too. Then there's a huge chance that you rule out a future rich in happiness and success. 'See? Typical: that's what always happens to me!'

Yes, indeed. Just like happiness.

25

On a roll

The core of Payroll Company comprises eight people. They are all good at what they do and they are all in the right place: where they can make their strength count.

All the processes within the company are heavily automated and are summarized in an operations blueprint, which we check every six months. We work on the basis of direct debit within two days, and we also pay our employees within the same period. We can print out a profit and loss account at any moment, any hour. We have millions in cash, no borrowed money and no amortization of debts. And I am dispensable. That was one of my main motivations when setting up Payroll Company. Because a company should be bigger than the people who work there.

Payroll Company is not the direct result of my entrepreneurial activities, but of my personal growth. I would never have achieved this growth if I hadn't first made the mistakes that brought me to my knees and forced me to look at myself and my motives and to work systematically on change. I have never been so conscious of myself as during this process. I had a vision of the future, I took the path that would lead me there, was open to whatever I encountered on the path and remained critical of myself without being judgemental.

In 2004, as I previously recounted, the temping agency took me on as an intermediary. In just six months I doubled the turnover of the branch where I was working. I arranged the secondment of our temping staff by simply contacting a company and asking whether people could come and work there. I had also applied this practical method when I was a franchise operator, and at the time it had brought me success there, too. The fact that my entrepreneurial activities had later degenerated into personal bankruptcy wasn't due to this quality, although the pressure of circumstances had steadily increased my fear and passivity.

Now I was a branch manager with a salary that I didn't receive myself. My performance bonus went straight to the bankruptcy administrator. There was something I noticed: I wasn't the only person working at this and similar temping agencies who earned a good income. The money for expensive business premises at A1 locations and high-earning managers had to be earned back by the temping staff. Hadn't I myself been sailing in a smaller but comparable boat? (One that had now sunk). Thirty full-time employees and no work. What do you do when you can no longer pass on your costs to the clients? I hadn't done enough, in any case, and I went bust.

As a branch manager I had daily contacts with my clients. They found our temping staff expensive too, but they needed the flexibility provided by the tempting agency and so they had little choice. Now that would be nice, wouldn't it? A temping agency with reasonably priced staff? A lean, mean and recession proof organization?

For what reasons do you lose clients? Because you're too expensive or because you make mistakes. So the ideal company applies low rates and doesn't make any mistakes. What do you need in order to do that? A perfect back office and a perfect administrative system. And what else? Fast payment by clients, enabling you in turn to apply the low rates and thus relatively narrow margins. So what's the best method then? Direct debit on a weekly basis.

And this was how, stone by logical stone, I built the image of the ideal organization in my mind, based on the lessons I had learned. I tried to imagine it down to the details. Was I the man, for instance, to lead an ideal organization like that? While the picture was taking shape, in 2005, I was convinced this wasn't the case. Be an entrepreneur? Never again. I was in a debt restructuring programme and the wounds of my bankruptcy were still far from healed.

Ideas have the urge to take on physical form. They don't want to remain in the realm of thought, but to live and to take shape. And to do this they have to leave the world of ideas, move beyond the head.

I discussed my ideas with like-minded people. One of them was the friend who had invited me to the Buddhist centre where I had experienced my visualization session. These people embraced the concept and shared the costs for setting up a private company with limited liability, Payroll Company. The friend who had taken me to the seminar became interim director. The new company had to be brought up to speed in commercial terms, they said, and they needed me for that task. That was a problem. I knew the plan was good and that it could be successful, but... I didn't have the courage. One of the wounds I now bore was the idea that I was a bad entrepreneur. The fear of failure was still anchored deep within me.

I had already had my first visions of a better future. I had walked around the house of my dreams but I hadn't yet reached the point, for instance, where I printed and wrote out the cheques that would guide me with concrete steps into the future.

A hefty dose of (self-)persuasion was needed before I finally resigned as branch manager at the temping agency. This step was unavoidable due to the non-competition clause that formed part of my contract. At that specific moment I had gained enough self-confidence to know that I could get a new job if I needed to.

In October 2005, after six months of getting over my fear, I began work as a sales employee for the company I had dreamed up myself. Payroll Company was a private company without personal liability. I received a salary: a minimum wage that was paid into the debt restructuring programme.

After a few months we needed to recruit a new employee for the bookkeeping. In the past I had shown pretty conclusively that I wasn't good at bookkeeping. Now a young lady by the name of Danielle came to the interview.

'Why should we employ you?' I asked.

'Because I want to be the best at what I do,' she answered.

That was the best answer she could have given. She was good at things that I'm bad at, and she really did turn out to be the best at what she did. And so Payroll Company began to experience success.

It seemed the future was in something of a hurry. A few months after I took up my new job the interim director decided to become a trainer and coach. I was devastated that he was leaving, but that's how it was. I had the opportunity to acquire twenty percent of the company.

I no longer wanted to be an entrepreneur, but I did have a dream. I dreamed of my own house, a new future. That's why it's so important to have a clear vision of what you want. And so once again I took a risky step.

I asked my parents to loan me money – 40,000 euros – even though I was just emerging from the debt restructuring programme. That was insane, inconceivable – unless you were me, and cherished my dream and conviction. My father had warned me and when it all went wrong he had still helped me. And now? He helped me again, although I still had an enormous moral and financial debt to him. I was able to persuade him because I was so resolutely convinced of my dream. But I told him that I couldn't guarantee anything.

Not long after this I bought out another shareholder. When I came home after completing this step, I had such an attack of nerves that I ran straight to the toilet and threw up.

After a relatively short time I owned sixty percent of the shares. I bought the other forty percent of Payroll Company at a later date. The shareholder received a good return on investment: about twelve thousand percent in three years.

And Aqil, the man who never wanted to be an entrepreneur again, was back in business.

There's no such thing as failure!

'But what if reality doesn't seem to match your dream? Realize that doubts have their place too, and you won't achieve everything you aim for. Take a look at the steps you've taken and still plan to take. Adjust your concept if necessary, without betraying or abandoning it. Because one thing is certain: you are already realizing your dream, right now. There's no such thing as failure!'

26

Birds of a feather

Thanks to Payroll Company I could now make a good job of what I'd previously messed up. And because I'd devoted so much energy to examining myself and to reading books that went along with this activity, I was willing and able to really do it, and with the right motivation. A hidden fear of failure, to give one example, was no longer the motor for my decisions. And so recognizing my own strengths and weaknesses no longer formed a threat to my ego. As a result I was able to involve others in my dream and my goals. Their qualities supplemented and complemented mine.

A few years ago I started thinking about which people in my life I wanted to have more contact with, and which people I would prefer to see less. Who did I want around me, and who didn't I want? I found I preferred people who were consciously engaged in making something of their life, who were successful in the area where I wanted to be successful too, or who were the best at what they did. Because if you want to receive advice that's worth listening to and that will help you on your path, you should ask the people who have achieved what you dream of. After all, they know how they managed it.

Some of these people became my best friends.

Gathering people around you who are better at something than you are, or have achieved something that you too would like to achieve, is an important step to success. And if you are going to look for people like this, seek out the very best you can find. You can probably learn the most from them. I had looked carefully at myself and examined my strong and weak points. When I looked around me, then everywhere I saw people who could use their own strengths to complement me with their know-how and competencies. I didn't need to concentrate so much on developing new abilities, but instead could focus on the things I was good at.

As soon as I had bought my first batch of shares in Payroll Company I sought out the two best businesspeople in the north of the Netherlands. I had heard of them but I didn't know them, and it was a tense moment. How do you ask someone you don't know for help? By asking.

Both of them unreservedly said yes. Every three months they would assess my own performance and how the company as a whole was doing. Plans, figures, results... they studied every aspect of business success. After each session I came home exhausted. They scrutinized everything and in the evening I returned with more work than I'd had in the morning. Each time there was so much to improve... You see, that's the flipside of choosing the best: it can demand the utmost of you and that's what you must be prepared to give.

My pride in Payroll Company is equal to, or greater than, the pride I had felt in my first company. That earlier pride, however, was centred on myself, pumped up my ego and kept me wanting even more. Nowadays my pride is based mostly on the people around me and associated with Payroll Company. My strengths complement those of the others.

Together we form an organism that produces happiness and success. I form an independent part of this, one person among equals.

If every day I name three things that make me feel joyful and happy, then these may well be the names of those I have met, know and am privileged to work with.

And what about you?

27

Completing the circle

You don't have memories, you create them. Images of the past are not 'real time recordings' but reconstructions. Just like you create and charge up your expectations of the future.

Memories are timeless, just like images of the future. You can recall an event and in doing so experience the feelings and images with great immediacy, but a different, more rational kind of effort is required to locate these in all time.

My story about Payroll Company belongs to the past. Because in the meantime I have departed from the company that I love. During the required visit to the public notary I cried like a child. I was saying farewell to the dream I had built, which had meant to much to me and had brought me so much. I was also saying farewell to the people who had helped me to shape the company.

Payroll Company was born from the lessons I learned after my bankruptcy. The birth was the physical, wonderful result of a dramatic mental and physical voyage of discovery. The discovery of myself, of my values and of my view of the world. A view I had been able to change, after which I was also able to change the world immediately around me. Payroll Company had taken on form and structure and this form and structure had been increasingly anchored in their own reality. But had the structures now become too constricting for me, a dreamer and a builder? The company had come of age and in doing so had outgrown me.

I had built up Payroll Company over the space of seven years. These years too had been an important part of my life. Did I want to keep doing the same for the next seven years, or was I seeking new goals and tasks for my future? So I sat down, thought about it and visualized.

Personal circumstances that I'll talk about in the epilogue strengthened my desire to reassign my priorities. Payroll Company was my brainchild, the realization of my dream – the proof that there's no such thing as failure and that you can rise from the ashes of your existence. It was a point of focus in my life and I devoted much of my time and energy to it. What would happen if I could no longer channel this time and energy in a wholehearted way?

I drew my conclusion. My following decision, however tough it was, was made easier by the fact that Payroll Company would get the best possible new owners. Remember, gather people around you who excel at what they do.

And so with the sale of Payroll Company the story of the sailor who became a millionaire would seem to get a nice and fitting end. It's a success story in which the hero (hi, that's me ☒) passes through the deepest valleys to ultimately attain the heights. But actually that isn't the whole story, but just a short chapter. For me it's less important than the real significance of Payroll Company and the value I recognize in everything I experienced on my path. Less important than what I've learned from and for myself, and now want to share with the world.

There's no such thing as failure.

My story is far from over.

It actually begins – and ends – with…

28

Myself, at last

There I stand, on stage, being applauded by an audience of entrepreneurs. I look for Sascha's face, can't find her, but know she's there with me. I'm happy. I'm successful. The cameras are recording it all.

Is it me they're photographing, or am I just the face of Payroll Company, the company that was successful from the word go? It's the latter, of course. I'm not on stage to be applauded for my personal growth and development, but for one of the achievements that resulted from this.

Entrepreneurship implies the taking of initiatives. I always took initiatives, but not always on the basis of strength. I worked hard, too hard, and my biggest motive was to avoid failure. I had something to prove – I thought. And because I didn't want to fail, I forgot to win.

The price I paid for my entrepreneurship and my personal growth included several difficult years and quite a lot of money. My bankruptcy made me small and nowadays I have no need or desire whatsoever to pretend to be bigger than I am. In the quest for myself I thought for a while that I would need to be a tough businessman in order to survive. But that's not how I am. I'm just Aqil. I want to help people and make them happy. Actually I'm a fairly nice person, and nice people too can work efficiently and earn money.

The bankruptcy made me a risk-avoider and so nowadays I think long and hard about things. If I then decide to do something, I go for it and I work consistently towards my goal without deviating too much from my course. Besides this, I'm trusting enough and optimistic enough by nature to run the risk of becoming opportunistic, meaning that I can leap on every opportunity that presents itself. Not that I want to squeeze the last drops out of the lemon, because now I understand that these last drops will be particularly sour. So in this respect I'm less greedy than I used to be.

But on the other hand I'm fairly resolute in comparison to the early days. I have the courage to say what I think, while I used to think up excuses and beat about the bush. If other people start presenting me with excuses, then I don't kick them out but I do point out what they're saying. By being honest to myself I can choose how I react or what I decide. I'd say that's something I've earned over the years.

Something else I have come to believe is that sincerity and realism aren't compatible with a general consensus or compromises. I know what will happen if I make wrong decisions, so I want these decisions to be pure. Maybe it's still a result of fear...

The most important development I have undergone is that, over the years, I have gained a totally different understanding of the term 'fail'. It has lost its power and now I no longer believe in failure itself. The only true failure involves not doing what you want. And that's why my fear of failure, which still exists, forms a reason for doing the things I do as well as possible, and not to neglect them.

Two little white socks triggered this and much more self-insight.

They made me realize how grateful I was for what I actually had, instead of focusing my mind on what I had lost. The two white socks freed me from the burden of all-inhibiting fear and self-criticism, enabling me to give my life a new direction. A direction I defined myself. With a goal I wanted to achieve. In a way that I chose. Those two little socks were my paradigm shift: a sudden change in my way of seeing things and my thought patterns.

I was overcome by gratitude. Gratitude set free by two little white socks. I had never experienced anything as intense before. It was like a huge wave of love. Later I became aware of how this interlinked with the 'how'. I knew how I was going to do it. The scales fell from my eyes. I was blind and now I see. And as soon as I was able to bid farewell to my fears and the accompanying fallacies, success found me with surprising speed.

Can you take happiness and success for granted as soon as you feel you have achieved them? On the wall of my office there's a poster of the Titanic, the unsinkable ship that sank. Because if you start believing you're invulnerable, that's when things really get dangerous. Today's success must never be your final goal. A few years ago I saw a therapist. Things seemed to be going too well. That made me afraid because, I thought to myself, soon things will be going wrong again... This fear proved unfounded, but it still plays a role in my life and I'm grateful that I have it.

A few times a year, or as soon as I get 'bellyache', I check my priorities and see whether I'm dividing my attention properly between work, family and friends. Sometimes I sit down and create a mental image of my present and future. I do this as soon as I feel the need. If I'm not feeling too happy, have a problem, have been satisfied for too long, or think: what now?

Twice a year I go off by myself and attend a meeting or seminar to strengthen, renew or reconfirm my personality and insights. At these times I invest in myself, because ultimately I'm the one who needs to function to the best of my abilities.

And every day I give myself a solid dose of AC/DC, Aerosmith, Guns N' Roses or Afrojack. I'm happy and enthusiastic by nature, but music peps me up even more. As does a good round of thumping and drumming on my shoulders, chest and legs, with accompanying caveman grunts. Believe me, it's better than any pills! And if I start getting overenthusiastic, then I've got another resource. Breathe in through the nose. Fresh air in. Breathe out through the mouth. Dark air out. In. Hold...

Out.

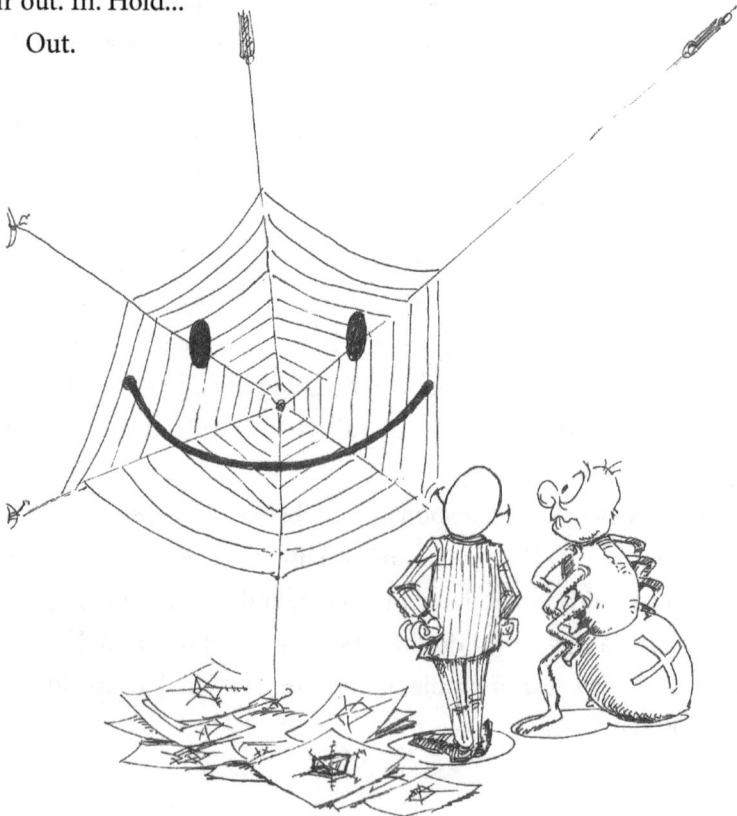

Steps

You can decide to be happier, healthier and more successful than you are now, or even think possible right now. Everyone who wants to realize a dream can do it. There are basic principles, prerequisites and techniques for doing this. Take the first step. If even I can achieve what I want, then you can certainly do it too!

Work out why you want something. This gives you the motivation to really make a change in your life. The reason why determines the initiative and the strength with which you head for your goal. The next step is to discover how you want to do it.

Say 'yes' to some things that make you feel uncertain and involve the possibility of failure. Fear is a great starting point for exploring and extending your boundaries. You're a fool if you know no fear, but you're a hero if you overcome it. And you're wise and on the path to happiness and success if you are able to recognize it.

Realize your reasons for being grateful. Without this realization your life will be governed by discontent and you will have neither the

passion to achieve what you want nor the will to dream. Of course this doesn't mean gazing into nothingness in pure rapture, because a certain amount of dissatisfaction moves you to act. Just never forget to be grateful.

Visualize your ideal future. What does it look like, how does it feel, sound, taste and smell? See yourself at the centre of this future. Anchor the image in your head and your heart. Make it more real than the reality around you. And rest assured: the image is already real, it just needs a while to be realized in concrete terms.

Change your actions and thoughts now. The big ones and the small ones. If you don't like something, change it or change yourself. Chest out, shoulders back, chin up, and your attitude to the world regains strength. By changing your actions, you also change your thoughts and beliefs. It begins with words. Just like the imagination, they form a powerful motivator and a dangerous instrument at the same time.

Recognize your hidden fear. Fear is a sly and underhand counsellor. It will whisper in your ear that it's better to abandon your dream, not take any risks and sit down with a bag of crisps to watch Fear Factor. So don't let fear tell you what to do, but recognize it as the true origin of your 'sensible thoughts'.

The right decision is not always easy, so ignore well-meaning advice. Those who love you want to shield you from pain, disappointment and other hardships encountered on an unfamiliar path. Decide for yourself whose advice you will follow and which things you will ignore. Ultimately there's only one person who knows what you are

capable of, and that's you.

Develop yourself. Learn, read and listen. Look at yourself with someone else's eyes. Work on yourself. Become aware, be aware, remain aware.

Choose and follow the right direction. How do you know which direction to take? By considering what makes you feel happy and joyful and choosing the route that will take you there. How do you choose the route? By fixing a grand, compelling point on the horizon and then defining the realistic goals that can get you there.

Set your goals. Define your aims. Without aims life is... aimless. Visualize them, feel them, with no limitations. Reality will impose the limitations by itself, so no need to worry about that. And of course: don't be afraid of failure, because there's no such thing. You might get frustrating or annoying results but these too contain something new and valuable. The only failure is not doing what you want.

Act on the basis of initiative and strength. Look at yourself and see what kind of dynamism and flow determine your actions. When you act on the basis of initiative and strength,
many objections disappear by themselves. Then you can focus on your goal instead of on your objections.

Be prepared for chances. A chance is an opportunity that presents itself and that leads you to success. The better prepared you are, the more often you see opportunities. Such chances present themselves every day, and you encounter the chance of a lifetime at least once every two weeks. Seeing them requires an open mind.

Seek out people with qualities different to and better than yours. Gathering people around you who are good at something, or have achieved something that you too would like to achieve, is an important step to success. And if you are looking for people like this, seek out the very best you can find.

Today's success must never be your final goal. Compare your performance with a sensible diet: you adjust your lifestyle and thus get rid of cumbersome ballast. Once you've achieved a healthy target weight you maintain the lifestyle you've established. Keep up the training, preferably with a friend, and watch out for the pitfalls that accompany success.

There's no such thing as failure!
And what if reality doesn't seem to develop like in your dream? Realize that feelings of doubt are real, too, and that not everything you aim for is going to succeed. Follow the steps you've mapped out. Adjust your image of the future, without abandoning it or constantly calling it into doubt. Because one thing is certain: you are already realizing your dream, right now. There's no such thing as failure!

Epilogue

While writing this book I received two pieces of bad news. One involved my wife Sascha, the other my mother. It transpired that my mother was terminally ill. In the meantime she has passed away.

During the period of my mother's illness, in which Sascha's ailment also came to light, I resigned from various managerial positions. Moreover I decided I would no longer hold chief responsibility for Payroll Company. I gave priority to Sascha's recovery.

Sascha has a frightening ailment. At that time, from one moment to the next and almost without warning, she could lose consciousness. Sometimes this happened once a week, sometimes twice a day. And when it happened, she fell over without being able to support herself – which resulted in things like bruising and even concussion. We didn't know what the illness was or why it appeared so suddenly. And we also had no idea whether it would get better by itself, or get worse.

We went to see medical specialists in various hospitals, who diagnosed epilepsy. But despite many examinations they had no explanation, let alone cure, for the black-outs. After months of increasingly frustrating hospital visits I decided to call on the help of friends and acquaintances. They shared my conviction that if you're looking for something good, you should seek the best. In this case our quest took us to Mayo Clinic in Rochester, Minnesota, USA. 'When can you guys come and how long can you stay?' they asked us when I called the clinic. 'As fast as possible and for as long as necessary,' was our answer.

A week later Sascha and I took a flight across the ocean.

At Mayo Clinic they repeated all the examinations already carried out in the Netherlands, and added some new ones. And this time they got a result almost immediately. Sascha's epileptic attacks, which were relatively mild, caused her heart to stop beating, which in turn meant that her brain didn't get enough oxygen. This explained the black-outs and her falling over. There was no cure for the epileptic attacks but they could do something about the resulting heart disorder. The doctors at Mayo Clinic gave her a pacemaker and so removed the life-threatening aspect of her illness. Now when Sascha has an attack she loses consciousness for a short time but she doesn't fall over so often.

These events experienced by Sascha and myself made me truly grateful for the first time that I had money. Money had already symbolized my ability to look after my family, and now it also secured Sascha's health. Money has a financial value and can be converted into other things, but the degree of happiness you achieve is determined by the goal you strive for and the value that you yourself attach to this.

Every day I name three things that make me happy and grateful.

Inspiring books

If you're aiming for increased happiness and success, I can recommend a number of books that I read and that helped me to see myself and the world around me in a new way. Here's a selection.

Dan Ariely, *Predictably irrational. The Hidden Forces that Shape Our Decisions.*
Leo Bormans, *The World Book of Happiness.*
Richard Branson, *Screw It, Let's Do It.*
Ivan Misner, *Truth or Delusion.*
Stephen R. Covey, *The Seven Habits Of Highly Effective People.*
Werner T. Küstenmacher, Lothar J. Seiwert, *Simplify Your Life.*
Dalai Lama, *The Art of Happiness.*
Jack Canfield, *Chicken Soup for the Soul.*
Ali Niknam, *Ondernemers hebben nooit geluk. ('Entrepreneurs Are Never Lucky')*
Anthony Robbins, *Unlimited Power.*
Jonathan Bowman-Perks MBE, *Inspiring Leadership.*
Ben Tiggelaar, *Dream, Dare, Do: Managing the most difficult person on earth: yourself.*
Ben Tiggelaar, *Can Do! How to achieve real personal change and growth.*
Tijn Touber, *The Secret of Genius.*
Paul Fentener van Vlissingen, *Ondernemers zijn ezels ('Entrepreneurs Are Jackasses')*

Hello?

Are you still there?

OK, obviously you haven't yet put the book aside and set off excitedly to realize one of your dreams. So write down one which you would like to come true. Select one action or undertaking which you know would make your life better, more enjoyable, happier, richer or healthier if you were to do it and succeed in it. Now write down the reason why you don't do it. And now draw a thick line through this reason and underneath write in big letters: 'BULLSHIT!'

I wish you all possible happiness and success!

www.ingramcontent.com/pod-product-compliance
Lightning Source LLC
Chambersburg PA
CBHW020517100426
42813CB00030B/3275/J